ERA OF EXPLORATION

THE RISE OF LANDSCAPE PHOTOGRAPHY
IN THE AMERICAN WEST, 1860-1885

Nature is but an image of wisdom,

the last thing of the soul;

nature being a thing which doth only do,

but not know.

PLOTINUS
Quoted in Ralph Waldo Emerson,
Nature, 1836

ERA OF EXPLORATION

THE RISE OF LANDSCAPE PHOTOGRAPHY
IN THE AMERICAN WEST, 1860-1885

WESTON J. NAEF

in collaboration with

JAMES N. WOOD

with an essay by

THERESE THAU HEYMAN

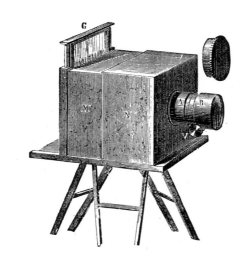

ALBRIGHT-KNOX ART GALLERY

THE METROPOLITAN MUSEUM OF ART

Distributed by NEW YORK GRAPHIC SOCIETY, BOSTON

This project is supported by a grant from the
National Endowment for the Arts
in Washington, D.C., a federal agency.

LIBRARY OF CONGRESS CATALOGING IN PUBLICATION DATA

Naef, Weston J.   1942-
  Era of exploration.

  Bibliography: p.
  1. Photography—Landscapes. 2. The West—Description and travel—Views. I. Wood, James N., joint author. II. Title.
TR660.N24   779'.36'9178   75-9694
ISBN 0-87099-128-0
ISBN 0-87099-129-9 pbk.

TITLE PAGE:

Simple wet-plate camera for field use. Woodengraving in J. Thomson, ed.,
A History and Handbook of Photography, *1877*

Designed by Peter Oldenburg
Composition by York Typesetting Co., Inc.
Printed by Rapoport Printing Corp.
Binding by Sendor Bindery, Inc.

Contents

Foreword

The museums that jointly produced this book and the exhibition from which it grew are themselves products of the "era of exploration." The foundings of the Buffalo Fine Arts Academy in 1862 and The Metropolitan Museum of Art in 1870 were expressions of the intellectual and educational ambitions of the same period that produced the great geological and geographical surveys. The establishment of Yellowstone, the nation's first national park, and the coming of age of landscape photography in the American West soon followed.

It is significant that our two museums are located in parks designed by Frederick Law Olmsted, who saw the newly discovered wilderness, like the fine arts, as a resource to be preserved "for public use, resort, and recreation." In addition to his responsibility for Delaware Park in Buffalo and Central Park in New York, Olmsted served as the first superintendent of Yosemite. His sensitivity to western landscape photography is evident from his personal collection of C. E. Watkins's views of Yosemite.

We are grateful to the National Endowment for the Arts, whose grant to the Albright-Knox Art Gallery made possible the exhibition. Its quality and that of the book would have been substantially less without the cooperation and support of John J. McKendry and his staff in the Department of Prints and Photographs at The Metropolitan Museum of Art. *Era of Exploration* is an outgrowth of the research and long interest in nineteenth-century landscape photography on the part of Weston Naef, Assistant Curator of the Department of Prints and Photographs at the Metropolitan. Mr. Naef and James Wood, Associate Director of the Albright-Knox Art Gallery, selected the photographs, organized the exhibition, and wrote the book, with the exception of the essay on A. J. Russell, contributed by Therese Thau Heyman, Senior Curator of Prints and Photographs at The Oakland Museum. Mr. Wood wrote the piece on Timothy H. O'Sullivan, and Mr. Naef is responsible for the remainder of the text. Their efforts are the realization of a cooperation between our two institutions that should serve as a model of its kind.

ROBERT T. BUCK, JR., *Director*
Albright-Knox Art Gallery

THOMAS HOVING, *Director*
The Metropolitan Museum of Art

Preface

Gallery walls have limitations that can be compensated in a book. However, the printed page also transforms photographs. The mammoth-plate photographs of Watkins, Muybridge, and Jackson can only be properly viewed as framed on the wall, and when reduced to the size of a book page—even an ample one—they inevitably lose some of their grandeur. But the achievements of early landscape photography are not limited to the mammoth-plate views, and, indeed, the great majority of landscape photographs are actually preserved as stereographs, which are stripped of their three-dimensional presence when shown on either the wall or the page.

In the reproductions an attempt has been made to respect the relative scale of the original dimensions. The Introduction and biocritical essays are illustrated, where possible, with halves of stereo pairs reproduced the same size as the originals. The full-page plates, on the other hand, are made from larger photographs; the largest horizontal images represent mammoth-plate views. The majority of landscape photographs are horizontal, but those that are not unfortunately suffer the limitation of the page height. Where mammoth-plate verticals and horizontals appear on facing pages, the vertical has been given maximum space, and the horizontal has been scaled proportionately.

Abbreviations have been used in the captions to indicate the size and source of the photograph reproduced. The size abbreviations, given first, are those used in sales catalogues issued about the time the negatives were made. Tables listing the abbreviations for the standard sizes and photograph sources follow. All photographs are albumen prints from collodion negatives unless otherwise stated in the captions. The majority of the plate illustrations have been reproduced from printers' negatives made directly from the original albumen prints so that the highest possible fidelity could be maintained. The titles and identifying numbers used are, where possible, the photographers' original captions. No attempt has been made to emend their idiosyncratic phrasing; states and locations, where missing, have been supplied by the authors.

The book is not a survey of western landscape photography, and in our more selective approach regrettable omissions were necessary. The photographs from the J. W. Powell Survey have been neglected, primarily because the most significant photographs produced under its auspices are ethnographic rather than landscape, although vast numbers of geological studies were made. The enigmatic William Bell, who worked with the Wheeler Survey for the 1872 season, has also been represented in merely a token way in spite of our admiration for his work. Photographs by many competent landscape photographers active after 1870 in California and Colorado have also been passed over with little more than a mention.

Both the exhibition and this publication, a joint venture of the Albright-Knox Art Gallery and The Metropolitan Museum of Art, required the willing cooperation of many individuals and institutions. The Albright-Knox administered the project from the research phase through the preparation of the manuscript and coordinated the traveling exhibition. The Metropolitan contributed the expertise of its curatorial and publications staff and executed aspects of the exhibition design.

An immense debt is owed the librarians, curators, collectors, and researchers who made available for study the materials in their custody. Robert B. McNee, Director of the American Geographical Society of New York, lent O'Sullivan and Watkins photographs to the Metropolitan Museum for long-term study. Sinclair Hitchings, Keeper of Prints at the Boston Public Library, and his assistant, Eugene Zepp, gave much assistance in the early phases of research and pointed out the rich resources of Boston collections that otherwise would have gone unrecognized. Hilda Bohem opened the Boni Collection in the Department of Special Collections, Research Library, University of California at Los Angeles, to us before it was fully catalogued and generously granted our requests for study photographs. Archibald Hanna, Jr., of the Western Americana Collection at Yale University, and his assistant, Joan Hofmann, alerted us to photographs and documents that would surely have otherwise been overlooked and generously consented to the loan of the entire group of Russell photographs exhibited. Maude Cole and Peter Rainey of the Rare Book Room of the New York Public Library made that collection available, and Walter J. Zervas facilitated the loan of photographs. Ruth Brown, Librarian of the Academy of Natural Sciences of Philadelphia, lent the collection of W. H. Jackson photographs to The Metropolitan Museum of Art for long-term study and in so doing materially influenced Jackson's role in the book and exhibition.

Alfred L. Bush and Joe Rothrock of the Princeton University Library assisted us there; and John Barr Tompkins and Suzanne Gallup of the Bancroft Library of the University of California at Berkeley kindly supplied study prints in immense numbers, as did Gary Kurutz of the Henry E. Huntington Library and Art Gallery, San Marino, California. Joe Thomas, William Leary, and Douglas Thurman of the Audio Visual and Still Pictures Division of the National Archives of the United States, Washington, facilitated our study of the massive collection of landscape photographs there; Nellie Carico informed us of the holdings of the library of the United States Geographical Survey, Reston, Virginia.

John Szarkowski of The Museum of Modern Art offered us in conversation and through his writings fundamental perceptions on the art of landscape photography. Dennis Longwell of the same museum obliged our need to use the study room at awkward times, and Diana Edkins shared her research notes with us and was an eager conversant on troublesome points.

Robert Sobieszek and his staff at the study center of the International Museum of Photography at George Eastman House, Rochester, supplied countless study prints, drew attention to elusive material in the collection, and consented to the loan of Muybridge, Watkins, and O'Sullivan photographs.

Peter C. Bunnell shared his knowledge of the history of photography and made available the Princeton University Art Museum's collection of photographs. Van Deren Coke generously offered us his unpublished research on A. J. Russell and supplied us with study prints from the collection of the Art Museum of the University of New Mexico and from his own collection.

Allen Fern and Gerald Maddox of The Library of Congress made available the rich resources of the Department of Prints and Photographs there and consented to the loan of important pieces.

We are grateful to those whose notes and research supplemented our own. Anne Aubrey Brown visited many collections in the Boston area; Stephen Feldman researched in the National Archives and The Library of Congress; Elizabeth Glassman spent time on our behalf at the Museum of Natural History, New York; and Reka Forizs assisted us at the International Museum of Photography at George Eastman House and at Columbia University.

Robert Weinstein, Anita V. Mozley, and Robert B. Haas shared their knowledge of California photography; and Bill and Mary J. Hood generously opened their extensive files on photographers in Yosemite. Terry William Mangan of the State Historical Society of Colorado corresponded with us about the negatives of W. H. Jackson.

Members of the American Paintings Department of The Metropolitan Museum of Art were consistently helpful. John K. Howat, Curator of American Paintings, read parts of the manuscript, and Natalie Spassky, Associate Curator, was informative on matters related to American artists; Doreen Bolger, Chester Dale Fellow in the department, was helpful specifically in matters of the bibliography. James Pilgrim, Deputy Vice-Director for Curatorial Affairs at the Metropolitan, was a partner from the conception of the exhibition and contributed significantly at every stage.

The book would have been dramatically less ample without the support of Bradford D. Kelleher, Museum Publisher, whose enthusiasm never flagged when the authors' concept of the undertaking repeatedly expanded. The book benefited from the intelligent and gentle editorial guidance of Polly Cone. Her thorough reading of the manuscript through several revisions added structure and continuity when the threads began to fray, and her good judgment was exercised during the production phase.

Among the staff of the Albright-Knox Art Gallery specific thanks are due John D. O'Hern, Coordinator of Public Relations and Publications; Serena Rattazzi, Publications Assistant; Douglas G. Schultz, Assistant Curator; Jane Nitterauer, Registrar; Alba Priore, Assistant Registrar; Elizabeth Burney, Executive Secretary; and Norma Bardo, Secretary, who have each contributed in important ways to the success of this publication.

Staff members in the Department of Prints and Photographs of The Metropolitan Museum of Art have contributed in ways that exceed measurement. John J. McKendry, Curator in Charge, introduced us to the landscapes of Eadweard Muybridge and nurtured our love of the photograph. Janet Byrne, Curator of the department, shared her understanding of the nineteenth-century landscape, and Colta F. Ives, Mary L. Myers, Suzanne Boorsch, and David Kiehl each contributed in important ways. A. Hyatt Mayor, Curator Emeritus, read the manuscript and clarified many points of fact and logic. Edmund Stack and Max Berman, Departmental Assistants, and Carlo Cocaro and Robert Grams of the Paper Conservation Laboratory prepared the exhibition to travel. Margaret Dunwoody helped to prepare the manuscript, and Lisa Kernan ably proofread.

The enthusiasm, encouragement, and critical insights of Mary Meanor Naef and Emese Forizs Wood provided welcome reinforcement during the project's two-year evolution.

Without the support of these and many others our project could not have been accomplished; without the generosity of the lenders our task would have been impossible.

WESTON J. NAEF
Assistant Curator
Department of Prints and Photographs
The Metropolitan Museum of Art

JAMES N. WOOD
Associate Director
Albright-Knox Art Gallery

Credit abbreviations

ACC	Arnold Crane collection
AGS	American Geographical Society, New York
ALB	Alfred L. Bush collection
ANS	Academy of Natural Sciences, Philadelphia
BPL	Boston Public Library
CHMD	Cooper-Hewitt Museum of Design, New York
CHS	California Historical Society, San Francisco
DW	Daniel Wolf Collection of the Erving Wolf Foundation
FL	Frederick S. Lightfoot collection
HB	Mr. and Mrs. Harvey Brewer collection
IMP/GEH	International Museum of Photography at George Eastman House, Rochester
HEH	Henry E. Huntington Library and Art Gallery, San Marino, California
HU	Houghton Library, Harvard University, Cambridge
JW	Joan Washburn collection
LC	Department of Prints and Photographs, The Library of Congress, Washington
LL	Mr. and Mrs. Lewis Lehr collection
LW	Lee Witkin collection
MIT	Rare Book Collection, Humanities Library, Massachusetts Institute of Technology, Cambridge
MMA	Department of Prints and Photographs, The Metropolitan Museum of Art, New York
MOMA	Department of Photography, The Museum of Modern Art, New York
NA	National Archives of the United States, Washington
NPS	National Park Service, Scotts Bluff, Nebraska
NYPL	Rare Book Room and Local History Department, New York Public Library. Astor, Tilden and Lenox Foundations
OM	Department of Photography, The Oakland Museum
P	Private collection
PU	Graphic Arts Collection, Princeton University
RBD	R. Bruce Duncan collection
SU	Bender Rare Book Room and Museum of Art, Stanford University, Stanford, California
SW	Samuel Wagstaff, Jr. collection
TL	Thomas V. Lange collection
UCB	Bancroft Library, University of California at Berkeley
UCLA	Department of Special Collections, Research Library, University of California at Los Angeles
USHS	Utah State Historical Society, Salt Lake City
UT	Gernsheim Collection, Humanities Research Center, University of Texas, Austin
YU	Western Americana Collection, Yale University, New Haven

Plate-size abbreviations

CDV	Carte de visite on standard mount, 2½ x 4 in.; the photograph generally trimmed to no more than 2⅛ x 3½ in.
F	Full plate, 8 x 10 in. standard
H	Half plate, 5 x 8 in. to 6½ x 8½ in.
I	Imperial plate, 9 x 12 in. to 14 x 16 in.
M	Mammoth plate, 15 x 18 in. to 22 x 25 in.; 18 x 21 in. average
½P	Half plate, 3¼ x 4¼ in. to 4 x 5 in.
⅙P	Sixth plate, 2¾ x 3¼ in.
S	Stereograph, before 1868, on standard mount, 3⅜ x 7 in.; the photograph trimmed to 3 x 3⅛ in. After about 1873 ("cabinet" size), on standard mount, 4 x 7 in.

ERA OF EXPLORATION

THE RISE OF LANDSCAPE PHOTOGRAPHY
IN THE AMERICAN WEST, 1860-1885

Landscape Consciousness

2. A. J. Russell (?) in Carmichael's Camp, Bitter Creek (Utah?). About 1869. s. LC

Awareness of nature reached its zenith in Europe and America during the fifty-year period between 1830 and 1880. Interest in the outdoors had been growing since about 1800 but culminated in the paintings and poems[1] created at midcentury. Landscape consciousness was also expressed in the eagerness of scientists to learn about the form and structure of nature. Perhaps out of necessity and perhaps by accident the invention and rapid development of photography as a visual medium coincided almost exactly with the generally heightened interest in nature and the land.

This book and the exhibition it accompanies are about the landscape of the American West as revealed in photographs from between 1860 and 1885 —a period when photographs were made outdoors in great numbers for the first time.[2] The purpose and usefulness of outdoor photography was heralded by technical and esthetic developments that introduced a golden age of landscape photography. As a golden age it was very short-lived, spanning the productive lives of a generation and a half of photographers, and, like golden ages in other art forms, it was preceded by works of importance and was followed at the turn of the century by equally important landscape photographs made, however, under different artistic assumptions. Neither the antecedents nor the successors to the generation of 1865 were as ambitious in their aims or as intensely competitive for success.

The generation of 1865, the first persistent out-of-doors photographers in America, comprised men who were photographing by the end of the Civil

War and whose productive careers extended into the mid-1880s and early 1890s. Of these only a small number, most working in the West, devoted themselves to making landscape photographs, as distinguished from outdoor photographs of other motifs such as architecture, transportation, or portraits.

Landscape photographers of the 1860s and 1870s have often been labeled "documentary," since an important segment of the work was done under the auspices of the government surveys and expeditions and the railroads. Among those whose careers came under governmental or institutional patronage were Timothy O'Sullivan (Fig. 1), A. J. Russell (Fig. 2), and William H. Jackson (Fig. 3).[3] Two other important figures, Carleton E. Watkins (Fig. 4) and Eadweard Muybridge (Fig. 5), made landscape photographs on their own initiative. Those five men are the protagonists in the rise of Ameri-

1. T. H. O'Sullivan (r.), McDowell and Berry in Panama. 1870. s. ACC

3. W. H. Jackson Photographing in High Places (Tetons Range). 1872. s. ANS

4. C. E. Watkins among Banana Trees at Wolfskell's, Los Angeles. About 1880. s. MMA

5. E. J. Muybridge ("Helios"), on Merchant's Floating Dock, San Francisco. About 1869. s. MMA

can landscape photography, along with such supporting figures as William Bell, A. A. Hart, C. R. Savage, C. L. Weed, and others, all of whom worked in the trans-Mississippi West just before and for two decades after the Civil War. There were, of course, many other photographers working in the West at the time, but very few devoted even a small portion of their energy to photographing landscape. Significantly, there were few photographers anywhere in the United States doing such ambitious landscape work. Thus, the rise of American landscape photography is to a great extent a child of the Pacific, rising from adolescence to maturity in the West, although its seeds were rooted in the eastern states and in Europe.

The five photographers all came to the West from elsewhere. Watkins emigrated to California from upstate New York at about the time of the gold rush; Jackson came from New York State just

after the Civil War; while Muybridge was an emigrant from England photographing in California after the war. Others were temporarily transplanted West—O'Sullivan was brought by Clarence King's Fortieth Parallel Survey and A. J. Russell by the Union Pacific Railroad, both from New York. The photographic and other activities in which they were engaged were sometimes more like experiment and adventure than physical exploration.

Era of Exploration is a two-edged catchphrase, for it suggests the actual process of travel and movement which was required of photographers prospecting for worthy motifs; the movement of photographers often coincided exactly with literal exploration being accomplished by teams whose goal was to map, measure, and chronicle the empty expanses along the fortieth parallel and one-hundredth meridian, which was newly accessible by the transcontinental railroad in 1869. The phrase

also suggests the exploration of the outdoors via the camera by photographers working in the new wet-collodion process, which arrived on the scene at the very moment photographers began looking at nature with a new seriousness. Exploration and experiment went hand in hand for the first generation of landscape photographers.

Ideally an artist in any medium might expect to derive esthetic satisfaction as well as an income from his work, but landscape photography during the first epoch of photography in America, the daguerreian era (1839–1859), could offer a photographer neither. The vast majority of all photographs made before 1860 and extant today are portraits, done either in the studio or in portable, artificial environments created by itinerant portrait photographers. The problem for photographers (and for painters, too), having become comfortable in the studio, was to remove themselves outdoors

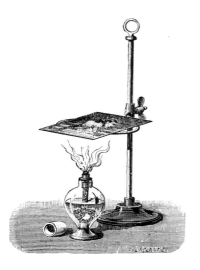

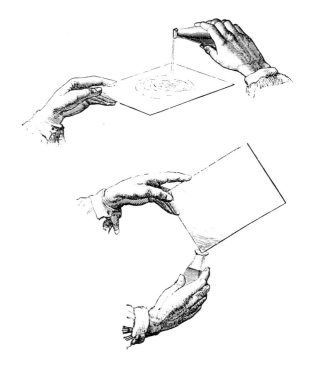

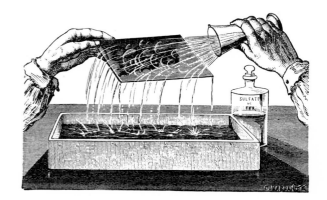

6. a. Gilding the daguerreotype plate. Woodengraving
    in J. Thomson, ed., *A History and Handbook of
    Photography*, 1877. MMA
    b. Mercurial developing box for daguerreotype

for the purpose of recording nature in its own midst. Taking the camera outdoors could have resulted either from the satisfaction of pressing artistic motivation of a purist sort or from the simple fact that a living could be made from doing so. Almost all outdoor photographs then were made by amateurs, many of them very talented, who had the time and money to pursue an entertaining but expensive diversion.[4] The rise of serious landscape photography was dependent on technology that made it profitable as well as satisfying. The key technical advance was the development of the glass-plate process, from which many identical prints of very high resolution could be made. The glass plate opened the possibility for publishing photographs and the consequent opportunities for photographers to make their livings by selling multiple prints from negatives. The budding commerce in photographs fueled the rise of outdoor work.

Many enormously successful daguerreian photographers continued to resist out-of-doors work simply because they had become so accustomed to the studio's controlled conditions. Transporting mercury, iodine, and sheets of silvered copper (Fig. 6) to the site of the photograph represented more of a cost and physical hardship than was worthwhile; most daguerreians stayed indoors while a hardy few worked outside regularly.[5] Moreover, the daguerreotype could not be easily reproduced except by an artist drawing a copy of the image on a plate or a stone. The eventual rise of landscape photography as an independent genre with its own esthetic premises was due in large part to the dissemination of the negative-on-glass process (Fig. 7), which made regular work outdoors an economic reality—a circumstance that did not take solid shape until after 1861 in the West. Photographers on the East Coast established a commercial trade in glass-plate photographs as early as 1854, the year Frederick Langenheim and his brother copyrighted their first set of outdoor photographs.[6] The most ambitious westward expansion in America made possible by the transcontinental railroad and the fascination the landscape of the West had always held for Easterners caused the West as a subject to dominate the rise of American landscape photography.

7. a. Coating the plate. First and second positions of
    the hands
    b. Washing the developed image

The technical obstacles to making outdoor daguerreotypes were sometimes less significant than the esthetic reasons for photographers' disregard of landscape. Between 1840 and 1855 most American painters worked in styles related to European romanticism, which encouraged imagination over naturalism; landscape paintings often emphasized the mood of nature rather than its literal appearance. Artists consistently defined the relationship of human beings to nature, and evidence of man, in the form of buildings, bridges, or vehicles was necessarily included, often as minute specks in large compositions. Thus, the picturesque quality of European and American landscape painting before 1855 was very distant from the truth-to-nature of a daguerreotype; daguerreian photographers were not induced to imitate what they saw in landscape paintings since a romanticized outdoor daguerreotype was technically very difficult to realize. Stock renderings done outdoors, such as Platt D. Babbit's group portraits on the edge of Niagara from his permanent studio there, relate to painting, but they are the exception rather than the rule in the era before glass plates.

The rise of a primitive style of landscape photography in America and around the world beginning after 1850 was intimately connected to changes in the painters' thinking which caused them not only to finally favor landscape but also to paint it more literally. The United States did not have an active school of landscape painting until the 1840s; what emerged then was a style derived from artists' concern with city views, portraits of gentlemen's estates, and transportation portraits (ships, trains, coaches), generally in a landscape environment. This evolved into a fully developed school of landscape for landscape's sake by the mid 1850s. Thomas Doughty (Fig. 8), Thomas Cole, M. J. Heade, Asher B. Durand, and George Inness often painted subjects within a considerable expanse of landscape but also generally included traces of civilization. The paintings of Thomas Cole and later of his student F. E. Church and of Albert Bierstadt began to

8. Thomas Doughty (1793–1856). A River Glimpse. Oil on canvas. About 1830. 30¼ x 25 in. MMA

15

represent landscape before the arrival of civilization.

The idea of wilderness unsullied by man became the actual subject of Asher B. Durand's painting Kindred Spirits (Fig. 9) of 1849. Durand painted William Cullen Bryant and Thomas Cole at the moment they discovered a particularly beautiful vale. The painting is a typical representation of the deep reverence for nature that prevailed as a sensibility at midcentury and which contributed in turn to the popularity of landscape photography. Early in his career Cole painted many landscapes that reveal his lifelong search for the pure state of nature. In a letter to Bryant, Cole said, "There is a valley reputed *'beautiful'* in the mountains a few miles south of the Clove—I have never explored and am reserving the delicate morsel to be shared with you. . . ."[7]

The appreciation of nature as a work of art is essential to the rise of landscape photography. Cole saw nature as art worthy of being experienced in the same way a connoisseur appreciates a masterpiece. Bryant's poetry, published widely in popular journals, also treated nature as art and contributed substantially to the increasingly widespread nature consciousness. The most significant journal of landscape art, *The Crayon*, asserted in 1855 that "untamed nature everywhere asserts her claim upon us, and the recognition of this claim constitutes an essential part of our Art."[8]

In order for photography to function as a visual equivalent to that poetic sensibility, a process was required that was replicable and that could also capture the minutiae of nature. That process was the negative on glass in its various patented forms, the earliest of which was albumen-on-glass method, and the most successful and long-lived of which was the wet-collodion-on-glass technique. The golden age of landscape photography coincided exactly with the dissemination of the wet-collodion process, which was more reliable than albumen for adhering light-sensitive salts to the glass negative.[9]

It is not easy to agree on exactly what "landscape" is in paintings made between 1845 and 1865. The same issue arises with the photograph. Any painting made to represent the out-of-doors might be said to be a landscape, and the same can be said of photographs. For the purposes of this book, those pictures that depict nature for its own sake will be called *pure landscape*. The golden age of pure landscape resulted from those photographers who went outdoors, not to photograph towns and cities, mines and mining, people in their occupations, or any of the numerous variations on daily life. This book treats that breed of photographer who focused his attention on nature itself as the primary subject. It is not concerned with those who occasionally made outdoor photographs, as many did, but rather with those who became deeply involved with the perception of land and nature and in whose photographs there is evidence of deep artistic conviction over a long enough period of time to have contributed substantially to a new manner of expression.

The popularity of studying nature in its purest form had much to do with discoveries in natural science and the wide dissemination of the new knowledge. Charles Darwin, who figures in the esthetics of landscape in a curious way, made his voyage around the world in the *Beagle* in 1832, and his writing on the origin of the species caused great public and private comment after it was published in 1859.[10] Louis Agassiz, the eminent anti-Darwinian, abandoned his family in Europe after studying with Alexander von Humboldt, whose seminal *Cosmos* first appeared in an American edition in 1851. Having published on tropical fishes and European glaciers, and having coined the term "ice age," Agassiz came to America, where he declared that "nature

was rich."[11] His essays on methods of study in natural history appeared serially in the *Atlantic Monthly* before their publication as a book. John Tyndall, the geologist who taught with Agassiz at Harvard, laid out the principles of geology for the United States, which was endowed with both the oldest known rocks and the youngest mountain ranges. Reports of Tyndall's investigations, along with those in botany, ornithology, and zoology, regularly appeared in popular journals and newspapers. Indeed, nature studies were so popular that the poet Ralph Waldo Emerson observed Agassiz's crowded classes and unsympathetically remarked that "something should be done to check the rush toward natural history."[12]

Photography ascended as the medium of picture making at exactly the same time the heightened popular appreciation of the natural orders occurred. Photography also played an essential role in integrating science with the traditional liberal arts, which, as Emerson's remark suggests, resisted accepting the relevance of science to painting and literature. Photography played a significant role in the initial courtship between science and the arts and the unfolding of American culture of the 1850s.

Photography and American Culture at Midcentury

One of the most influential and ambitious paintings to emerge from the new sense of naturalism in landscape was Frederic E. Church's Niagara (Fig. 10), first exhibited in 1857. In 1853 Church had set out with the financier Cyrus Field to retrace the itinerary of Alexander von Humboldt through South America with the southern cordilleras as their destination. Conceivably Church had read in *Cosmos* Humboldt's few remarks on the potential of photography for delineating remote regions, but it is unlikely that Church took any photographs in South America himself, although he collected professionally made views. Upon his return, however, he doubtless consulted photographs of Niagara Falls as models for his painting.[13]

The first published photographs of Niagara were made and offered for sale by Frederick and William Langenheim in 1854 (Fig. 11). William operated the camera and deserves credit as the first American landscape photographer whose work has survived. The Langenheims had photographed Niagara with daguerreian equipment in 1845 and knew that outdoor photographs were of little commercial use unless they could be multiplied more easily than daguerreotypes. Thus about 1850 Frederick Langenheim went to Europe, where he acquired the American rights to W. H. Fox Talbot's and Niepce de St. Victor's glass-negative processes, from which numerous highly resolved impressions could be made. Langenheim returned, having learned to make negatives using egg white to adhere the light-sensitive solutions to glass. He patented the process in 1850 under the name "Hyalotype."[14]

The Langenheims' 1854 stereoscopic views on paper—probably the ones Church saw—had an

10. W. Forest. Engraving after Frederic E. Church (1826–1900). The Great Fall—Niagara. About 1857. 27½ x 18 in. MMA

NIAGARA FALLS,—WINTER VIEW.

Canada side

TABLE ROCK.

F. LANGENHEIM'S PATENT, Nov. 19, 1860.

Entered according to Act of Congress, in the year 1856, by F. Langenheim, in the Clerk's Office of the District Court for the Eastern District of Pennsylvania.

11. Frederick Langenheim. Niagara Falls—Winter View.
About 1854. s. MMA

12. Brewster's stereoscope, model of about 1860.
Woodengraving in J. Thomson, ed., *A History and Handbook of Photography*, 1877. MMA

13. Twin-lens camera, showing dark slide and diaphragms

added virtue in their illusion of three dimensions. Humans perceive space through two eyes set about two and one-half inches apart, and each eye sees the world from a slightly different point of view; the two vantage points are fused in the mind to effect the perception of distance and space. When two photographs are made from two points the same distance apart as the eyes they too are fused in the mind and assume the illusion of three dimensions when seen through the stereoscope (Figs. 12, 13).[15] The stereoscopic images delineated nature with vivid naturalism, sometimes creating spatial and perspectival effects that would have been impossible in life. Stereoscopic photographs heightened the dramatic elements in nature and enhanced its appeal as a subject for paintings. The role of the stereograph in the general rise of landscape consciousness is enormous. It was soon adopted as a tool by certain artists, including Church; photographers utilized the more portable stereo camera

to make studies for their large-plate photographs (Fig. 118).

In 1855 Frederick Langenheim traveled the routes of the Reading, Catawissa, and Elmira railroads to again photograph Niagara Falls, making stereoscopic landscape views along the way.[16] The photographs he made of Niagara itself were so successful that he returned the following summer to photograph it without snow. The Langenheim stereographs pictured the falls with a heightened sense of space that revolutionized picture making. F. E. Church, like everyone else who saw the pictures, must have been overwhelmed; for the first time in photographs, one had the illusion of being on the precipice of the falls. Niagara is framed in typical camera fashion—very frontally, from the best point of view above the falls on the American side. The cataract itself would have been the natural focal point, as it was in Edward Hicks's painting of 1825 and in most other earlier renderings of

OPPOSITE PAGE:
15. A. S. Southworth and J. J. Hawes. Niagara Falls. Daguerreotype. About 1853. F. MMA

14. Alexander Hesler. Minehaha Falls, Minnesota Territory. Salt print from albumen negative. About 1856. F. MMA

MINEHAHA FALLS, MIN. TER.
Negative by A. Hesler.

the site. Photographs frame a composition with utter disregard for what is beyond the field of vision encompassed by the lens; the human eye records a much wider scope than the camera, and paintings most often encompass a span not available to the photograph.

Church's Niagara was among the most highly praised paintings of its time, commented on by critics as various as Mark Twain and the newspaper art columnists, who inadvertently approved the photograph as a painter's aid. Church himself apparently took note of this imprimatur, for in his subsequent work he made increasing use of photographs. Photography was often accused of leaving little to the imagination by artists who prized imagination over reason in the hierarchy of art forms prescribed in the ancient argument of the *paragone,* but Church's interpretation of Langenheim is the more compelling for what it leaves to the imagination in spite of its naturalistic detail.

Photography in the fifties began to exert its influence on the literature of nature as well as art. Alexander Hesler, a Chicago contemporary of the Bostonians Southworth and Hawes, went up the Mississippi River in 1851 in a journey similar to Southworth's and Hawes's pilgrimage up the Hudson to Niagara five years before. Hesler was primarily a portrait photographer and would continue to be so for the remainder of his career, but like other daguerreians of adventuresome spirit, he stepped from his studio on a few significant occasions. One of his landscape photographs is said to have influenced Henry Wadsworth Longfellow. Hesler arrived at the falls, called by the Indian name *Minnehaha,* and made a now-lost daguerreotype which he took back to his studio. It was exhibited and subsequently purchased by George Sumner of Boston. Sumner gave the daguerreotype to his brother Senator Charles Sumner, who in turn gave it to his friend Longfellow. The historian Robert Taft tells us that "over a year later Hesler received an autographed copy of the poem 'Hiawatha' as well as a letter in which Longfellow

stated that the incentive for his famous poem came after viewing Hesler's daguerreotype."[17]

In 1857, after he had abandoned the daguerreotype in favor of the replicable glass process, Hesler returned to Minnehaha to photograph the site he had helped make famous. He used the new albumen-on-glass process he had learned from Frederick Langenheim. The albumen process permitted the production of identical prints, which, unlike the daguerreotype original, could be used in their initial form for illustrations. Original prints of Hesler's new Minnehaha (Fig. 14) were made in the primitive salt-paper process that preceded albumen printing paper, and mounted into every copy of the *Photographic and Fine Art Journal* in 1857. The photograph was accompanied by the four lines from *Hiawatha* relevant to Hesler's picture and represented a dramatic new departure in book illustration.

> As we see the Minnehaha
> Gleaming, glancing through the branches
> As one hears the Laughing Water
> From behind the screen of branches?

The poem repeats twice the image "through the branches" and "screen of branches," an effect that may have been prominent in a photograph because of the tendency to create an artificial frame determined by the edges of the camera's lens. In the photograph overhanging branches take on the appearance of a screen at the edge of the picture, a compositional conceit unique to the camera lens. The excerpt from Longfellow contains a naturalism that might not have existed without the photograph and suggests a relationship between photography and literature similar to the interaction between painting and photography that resulted in Church's Niagara.

In the 1850s there was no firmly established school of American landscape photography. There were few isolated practitioners, and there were the beginnings of a movement in the work of Frederick Langenheim and others. For the most part landscape was a very subordinate activity for those photographers like Southworth and Hawes, whose far-reaching talents allowed any direction they chose. Given the vast range of motifs nature offered, they followed portraiture most consistently and most brilliantly. They had made penetrating red-plush parlor portraits of all the important people in Boston society, many of whom were also famous national figures: John Quincy Adams, Daniel Webster, and William Henry Harrison.[18] They also made a few extraordinary outdoor views, which demonstrate how the typical daguerreian studio contended with the out-of-doors.

Southworth and Hawes, either singly or together, visited Niagara Falls in about 1853 and photographed it in midwinter when it was frozen into a spectacular ice sculpture (Fig. 15); their Niagara daguerreotype is a portrait of nature controlling its own self-destructive energy, and it reveals the aim of most outdoor photographers of the era—to capture nature in a rare moment. Daguerreians were able to contend with the obviously monumental in nature but not with the flux and chaos, which would attract the dedicated landscape photographers of the 1860s and 1870s. Daguerreians were enticed out of their studios for newsworthy events, such as volcanic eruptions, fires, floods, and other disasters. On commission they would do portraits of buildings, animals, and vehicles, or any other subject that could remain motionless long enough to be photographed; however, the main attraction for the daguerreians were timely subjects like those that dominated the woodengraved newspaper illustrations. They avoided what might be expected to stay the same—mountains, vales, rocks, and trees, the essential elements of pure landscape. It was not, therefore, until the wet-plate era that a true school of landscape photography flourished, although the photograph at midcentury had already begun to exert an influence on the literary and artistic spirit of the times.

American Landscape and the European Antecedents

American art of the nineteenth century was frequently fertilized by ideas from abroad which grew into their own forms once transplanted. The case with photography was no different. Landscape photography, like landscape painting, developed in Europe before it did in America. However, by 1867/1868, C. E. Watkins had been awarded a medal for landscape at the Paris International Exposition. In 1874 Muybridge was praised by Dr. Hermann Vogel, Berlin's eminent professor of chemistry, the mentor of Alfred Stieglitz, and a landscape photographer in his own right. The same year Muybridge won the prize for landscape at the Vienna International Exposition, where it was noted that nothing like the size and rugged honesty of California's mammoth-plate landscapes had ever been seen in Europe. On extending his praise Dr. Vogel overlooked the European origins of the landscape esthetic and was apparently overwhelmed by the American use of mammoth plates (Fig. 94).

A pastoral manner of landscape photography evolved almost simultaneously in Britain and France during the 1850s. British photographers like Philip Delamotte, Roger Fenton, and Thomas Sutton used the paper-negative process during the early 1850s then converted to negatives on glass in the mid- to late fifties. Paper negatives produced photographs that had the softness of drawings or lithographs (Fig. 16), in contrast to the mirrorlike resolution of the daguerreotype. The early photographs of Gustave Le Gray, who worked in Paris, are typical of the pastoral style of European landscape. His view of a rocky landscape (Fig. 17) of about 1850 was made with a paper negative and is representative of the painterly quality of photo-

16. Thomas Sutton. Landscape in Jersey, England. About 1855. F. P

graphs before glass negatives. The picture is related in subject to an 1868 glass print by Timothy O'Sullivan (Fig. 18) of a rock formation in the Humboldt Range of Nevada. The comparison perhaps suggests more about the tremendous esthetic distance between the paper and glass processes than the differences between O'Sullivan and Le Gray as artists. O'Sullivan's photograph captures the myriad detail of nature from foreground grasses to the strata of the rocks. Le Gray, on the other hand, evokes the atmosphere and mood of nature rather than persuasive reality through details.

Between 1855 and 1859 albumen on glass began to be widely used in Britain and France, particularly for stereographs, and the portability of the stereo camera perhaps contributed to the rise of wilderness photography. Roger Fenton, a friend of Le Gray's when both were students in the atelier of Paul Delaroche in Paris, went to the backwoods of Wales (Fig. 19) and photographed landscape there.[19] Fenton's contemporaries on the Continent had much more grandiose subjects at their disposal, in the mountain regions of Savoy and the Alps, which gave rise to a school of wilderness photography of great relevance to photography as it would develop in California after 1861.

Friedrich von Martens, a German living in Paris, made technical advances in the daguerreotype process and made paper negatives of Mont Blanc that were exhibited at the Paris Universal Exposition of 1855.[20] Foremost among European photographers of mountains at the advent of the glass-plate process was Charles Soulier, who made glass stereoscopic views in partnership with C. M. Fer-

17. Gustave Le Gray. Landscape near Paris (?). Salt print from paper negative. About 1852. F. SW

18. T. H. O'Sullivan. Wave Rock, East Humboldt Mountains (Nevada). 1868. F. AGS

23

19. Roger Fenton. Pool on the Llugwy. About 1857. s. NYPL

20. Charles Soulier. Ice Formation. About 1860. s. MMA

21. Francis Frith. Mt. Horeb, Sinai. About 1860. F. MMA

OPPOSITE PAGE:
22. Samuel Bourne. Cascades on the Scinde River, Kasmir. About 1861. I. P

rier. Ferrier's works were immediately seen around the world in their identical glass stereoscopic mounts, which were distributed universally between 1859 and 1865. Soulier was gifted with a unique vision of landscape, which was transformed in his photographs into features that might be from another planet. His study of an ice formation (Fig. 20) becomes a metaphor of the most primordial aspects of nature.

Glass-plate photography allowed ambitious but practical projects by photographers who wanted to photograph the wilderness. European photographers from the daguerreian epoch had visited all corners of the world—Asia, Africa, the Near East, and North and South America—but the daguerreotypes had such limited usefulness for publication that few of the originals were even deemed worth saving. The first generation of glass-plate photographers, however, saw their photographs published and circulated around the world, providing a profit incentive for more ambitious photography campaigns.

In 1857 Francis Frith was sent to the Holy Land by the publishers Negretti and Zambra of London. His results were so successful that he went again in 1859.[21] Monuments of Egyptian and biblical civilizations dominated the first series, but the second focused on the biblical landscape of mountains, valleys, and oases of significance in terms of Christian and Judaic scripture (Fig. 21). From this campaign resulted over three hundred glass and paper stereoscopic views and enough six-by-eight-inch views to fill several volumes, all of which received worldwide distribution unlike any other photographs before them. The London *Times* called them the most important photographs "ever published."[22] They were used to embellish the first Bible illustrated with photographs. Frith's mammoth-plate views, made at the same time, received a curiously limited circulation.

In 1861 Samuel Bourne, an Englishman living in India, set out to photograph the Himalayas with the assistance of more than thirty servants to carry his bulky wet-plate equipment and provisions. Bourne had a finely developed landscape sense and used a nine-by-eleven-inch negative to accommodate the grandeur he encountered (Fig. 22). Bourne, soon to be in partnership with Shepherd, established a photography studio in Calcutta that sold prints from his 1861 negatives throughout the nineteenth century. The studio exists today, and prints are still made from Bourne's original negatives.[23]

Bourne's and Frith's journeys are only two examples from among many campaigns of photography instigated in the late fifties and early sixties. The importance of similar work has many times gone overlooked by even local historians. Photography became so prolific during the sixties that it was difficult to realize, once the record had been blurred by time, how significant was the twofold achievement of the pioneer wet-plate photographers who flourished twenty years after the invention

of the medium. They had not only set about accomplishing the first sustained body of outdoor work, which gave rise to the genus of landscape photography, but they were the first generation to see their photographs published and distributed to a wide audience. They were also the first phase in a future cycle in which photographs influenced other photographs (Figs. 46-52).

The most ambitious American exponent of this first rush to photograph outdoors was Carleton E. Watkins, a San Francisco photographer who had had made—presumably by a cabinet maker, as there were no camera factories—a mammoth camera for making eighteen-by-twenty-one-inch negatives (Pls. 1–4, 12). In 1861 he visited the recently discovered Yosemite Valley, a two days' journey southeast from San Francisco, where he had made a significant group of photographs of the wilderness. Little is known about Watkins's career before his first Yosemite trip except what is related by his biographer, since none of the pre-Yosemite photographs are known to survive. We are told that Watkins was a photographer before 1861, but for all intents and purposes his career began with the Yosemite photographs, which are the earliest extant work of the most prolific photographer working on the Pacific Coast in the sixties, seventies, and eighties. For most of the sixties he photographed wilderness landscape and little else. He shared his affinity for the outdoors with few other photographers anywhere in the country.

Watkins was not the first American photogra-

24. Worthington Whittredge (1820–1910). The Trout Pool. Oil on canvas. 1870. 36 x 27⅛ in. MMA

23. Frederick Langenheim. Marshall's Falls, near Del. Water Gap. About 1855. s. P

RIGHT:
26. Edinburgh Stereoscopic Company of New York. Unidentified landscape. About 1860. s. MMA

27. Deliss Barnum. Waterfall in the White Mountains. About 1861. s. MMA

25. D. Appleton and Co. Emporium of Stereoscopic Views, New York. About 1860. s. FL

pher to photograph landscape, but he was the first individual photographer working as an artist with a desire to become widely known for landscape work. In the East Frederick Langenheim had photographed a great deal of landscape beginning as early as 1854, but he did not methodically cultivate a personal style as Watkins did. Langenheim produced landscape views of picturesque places tourists visited (Fig. 23). He hoped to sell as many photographs as possible to recoup his substantial investment in the American patents for the albumen-on-glass process. His photographs are of intimate pastoral subjects—in contrast to the wilderness grandeur of Watkins's work—and echo the subjects of contemporary paintings (Fig. 24). Langenheim's career as a working photographer ended about 1860, which was insufficient time for him to explore any of his artistic premises to their logical conclusions.

Langenheim's contribution was to establish commercial landscape photography, which gave rise to competition about 1860 from other organizations, especially E. and H. T. Anthony, George Stacy, and D. Appleton and Co. (Fig. 25), all in New York. They hired photographers to work outdoors, thereby giving birth to the first generation of American photographers whose pursuit was outside the studio. Prior to the Civil War, landscape formed a substantial part of the catalogue of photographs offered for sale by the New York outlets. These were largely pastoral subjects (Figs. 26, 27) based on the styles of British and French photographs of the preceding decade. Eastern photographers resisted establishing their reputations on a single subject such as landscape. Photographic artists active before the Civil War, such as George Barnard, Deliss Barnum, F. B. Gage, T. C. Roche, John Soule, and many others based their reputa-

28. John Soule. Interior of Snow Arch, Tuckerman's Ravine, August 16, 1861. s. MMA

tions on general outdoor work which included city views, estate portraits, landmarks, architecture, and transportation pictures. They were pioneering outdoor photographers but not devoted to picturesque landscape as their main subject.

Perhaps as a result of Frederick Langenheim's early activity, Philadelphia came to have the first really defined school of landscape photography in the United States. The interest began there between 1854 and 1859, when Langenheim had the monopoly patent on glass negatives. As early as 1850 a group of Philadelphians was practicing landscape photography. Among them were Carey Lea, said to have made the first negative on paper in the United States; Coleman Sellers, whose writing popularized the new (1863) globe lens for landscape; and E. L. Wilson, editor of *Philadelphia Photographer*, which was biased toward landscape photography and was among the first publications to praise Watkins and Muybridge. Active in the mid-sixties were W. T. Purviance and John Moran, brother of the painter Thomas Moran, who would be associated with W. H. Jackson on the Hayden Survey in 1870. However, like a similar group in New York, the Philadelphia school was established very much on the model of European picturesque photography. Between 1859 and 1863 a Boston group began making and publishing landscape photographs. Among its most successful members were Barnum and Soule (Figs. 28, 29), who, like Watkins, combined an interest in landscape with a pursuit of city views.

29. John Soule. Photographic Camp, near Profile Lake (White Mountains). About 1861. s. LL

Western Adventurers Outdoors

30. Attributed to J. D. Hutton. Falls on the Yellowstone River. 1869. ¼ P. YU

The most picturesque landscape motifs of the Northeast—the White Mountains, the Hudson River Valley, and the waterfalls along the main rivers—were much photographed, some to the point of being hackneyed subjects by 1863. But the public continued to buy photographs of landscape, and photographers naturally looked West, where grand and new motifs were abundant. Access to the West was limited, however, until after the Civil War.

The government was a potential source for such photographs; the Treasury and War departments had used photography on some prewar exploring parties dating back to as early as the infancy of photography in 1842.[24] However, if success may be measured by a body of images esteemed or useful enough to survive to the present day, or by ones that merely exerted some measurable influence on those few who were privileged to see them, photography on expeditions prior to those of Col. F. W. Lander and Capt. W. F. Raynolds in 1858/1859, was a failure. Robert Taft, in his monumental history of American photography, notes a long succession of attempts by daguerreian and early glass-plate photographers to make photographs on exploring expeditions. From some of these, including the earliest—the Northeast Boundary Survey of 1842—emerged some viewable images, now lost; many other attempts were outright failures. The wet-plate photographs of J. D. Hutton (Fig. 30), who photographed with Raynolds,[25] exemplify the primitive results that characterized wet-plate expeditionary photography of the late fifties. Hutton's photograph also draws attention to the near-miraculous advances in photography over only three or four years that made possible the remarkable achievement of Carleton Watkins's 1861 mammoth-plate and stereo views of Yosemite (Pls. 1–5, 12).

31. W. C. Mayhew. Sitgreaves Expedition, July 26, 1850. Daguerreotype. H. RBD

32.
W. C. Mayhew. Dr.
Samuel Woodhouse,
June–July 1850.
Daguerreotype. 1/6
P. RBD

While wet-plate photography was in its infancy in the fifties, the daguerreotype was at its zenith. Very few, if any, daguerreotypes of landscape have survived from this epoch, a regrettable fact, since the daguerreotype would have been well suited to recording the minutiae of the western outdoors.

Of the few daguerreian images that survive from expeditions prior to Lander's, none are more typical than those made by W. C. Mayhew, who accompanied the expedition of 1st Lt. Lorenzo Sitgreaves to survey the Creek and Cherokee boundary in the Indian territory west of Arkansas (Fig. 31). On 26 July 1850 Mayhew made a daguerreotype of the members of the expedition around their tents, an image representative of what interested exploring parties—camp life, wagons, army forts, Indians, and evidence of Manifest Destiny in the westward march of civilization. The men were pleased to have themselves portrayed in the costume of exploration, hunting knives prominent, as in Mayhew's daguerreotype of Dr. Samuel Woodhouse (Fig. 32), who was on the Sitgreaves expedition.[26] Rarely did either daguerreians or the wet-plate artists of the late fifties photograph landscape for its own sake.

Landscape painters from the East were among the first to seek out exciting new landscape motifs in the West, and a few, like Frederic Church and Albert Bierstadt, saw the potential usefulness of photographs to the painter. In the spring of 1859 Bierstadt traveled west with Col. Lander's expedi-

tion, whose mission was to survey the practicality of a wagon road over the "south pass of the Rocky Mountains."[27] Bierstadt had a camera for making stereoscopic photographs, and, largely because his brothers were photographic publishers in New Bedford, Massachusetts, his primitive but vanguard photographs of 1859 have survived (Figs. 33, 34); nevertheless they exist in exceedingly small numbers, which indicates the nascent state of commercial photography in the fifties.

Bierstadt's photographs, while unimpressive visually, represent a key moment in American landscape consciousness as expressed in photographs. Bierstadt wrote to the editor of *The Crayon*, an important journal of Ruskinian thought, that "the mountains are very fine; as seen from the plains they resemble very much the Bernaise Alps. Their jagged summits, covered with snow and mingling with clouds, present a scene which every lover of landscape would gaze upon with unqualified delight. We have taken many stereoscopic views, but not so many of mountain scenery as I could wish owing to various obstacles attached to the process."[28] The obstacles of which Bierstadt wrote were faced by every photographer who attempted to make glass-plate views in the wilderness up to this time. Bierstadt's words also suggest his looking at mountains and landscape as works of art in their own right, as had Cole and Bryant earlier, a point of view articulated most visibly by the British artist and theoretician John Ruskin. Ruskin's thought underlay much of the fervid interest in landscape that rose in America at midcentury.

There were few cities close to majestic natural phenomena to support the work of independent outdoor photographers. But cities, paradoxically, played an important role in the development of wilderness photography and of outdoor photography in general. Prosperous cities near interesting motifs spawned the first generation of outdoor photographers, most of whom made landscape photographs occasionally aside from their general view work; few devoted themselves entirely to landscape, although some, like Alexander Hesler, sometimes did so. After Hesler and before the Civil War a local school of landscape photography rose in the upper Mississippi valley; the gallery of J. E. Whitney in St. Paul, Minnesota, supplied landscapes of wilderness areas to the East (Figs. 35, 36). The wealth of the upper Mississippi was based on fur trading and minerals, and the pros-

33. Albert Bierstadt. Devil's Gate, Passage of the Sweet Water River, Na. No. 75. 1859. s. NYPL

34. Albert Bierstadt. Sioux Village near Fort Laramie, Na. No. 72. 1859. s. NYPL

35. J. E. Whitney. Dalles on the St. Croix. 1860–1865. CDV. MMA

36. J. E. Whitney. Dalles on the St. Croix. 1860–1865. CDV. MMA

THE DALLES ON THE ST. CROIX.

37. A. S. Southworth. San Francisco. Daguerreotype. About 1853. H. MMA

sciousness to flourish. The gold rush of 1849 had naturally drawn photographers, including eastern photographers like Albert Southworth (Fig. 37), most of whom made portraits; but daguerreians set up their cameras outdoors in San Francisco more than anywhere else in the world. Robert Vance specialized in views of towns and mines and shipping scenes as well as portraits. G. R. Fardon, working in San Francisco as early as 1856, was one of the pioneers in the glass-plate technique. He conceivably learned the Langenheim process about the same time as Hesler did in Chicago. There is no record of Fardon's having photographed landscape, but his set of views around San Francisco is one of the earliest surviving sequences of photographs of any American city.[29]

The decade between 1849 and 1859 gave many San Francisco photographers the experience of working outdoors under semiprimitive conditions. Work around the city itself was no different from in cities anywhere except that the inherent picturesqueness drew more photographers outdoors. Those daguerreians in the gold fields accumulated experience working several steps from civilization but not quite under the primitive situations experienced by John C. Fremont and the other early expeditionary daguerreians. It was not long before an enterprising figure like J. Wesley Jones could turn his back on the obvious subjects drawn from life and daguerreotype the land itself.

Jones was the only daguerreian photographer working in the West who reportedly had a significant interest in landscape, although not one of his daguerreotype landscapes is known to survive. He traveled from San Francisco to St. Louis in 1851 photographing "scenery, curiosities, and stupendous rocks; embracing a vast collection of all that is rich and rare among the deep gorges."[30] Drawings after his daguerreotypes (Fig. 38) offer a tantalizing suggestion of the seminal role his work probably played in the genesis of a regional school of landscape photography. Jones was not necessarily artistically devoted to landscape, for his

perity fostered the growth of outdoor photography. However, the possibilities were more limited than those on the West Coast because the midwestern landscape itself was so much less dramatic.

San Francisco was the city most accessible to dynamic outdoor motifs of all kinds—ships, mines, architecture, and railroads—as well as awesome landscape. Not only was the city itself highly photogenic, but the landscape within a half-day's carriage ride was more spectacular than much to be seen in the East. San Francisco was the only wealthy urban center west of St. Louis prior to the transcontinental railroad. There were, of course, other towns and emerging cities, but they lacked the affluence that traditionally caused picture con-

daguerreotypes do not appear to have been inspired by a driving love of nature alone. Deeply interested in landscape, but more of a journalist, Jones hired experienced eastern artists to translate his daguerreotypes into paintings, which he used in a pantoscope lecture (Fig. 39) he gave on his travels to enthusiastic lyceum audiences.[31] The pantoscope was a painted diorama like a Chinese scroll, which, when unrolled across the stage, provided a continuous illustration of Jones's text. The disappearance of the Jones daguerreotypes is a tragic gap in the history of landscape photography in the West. Work so ambitious and so foresighted must have influenced the youthful generation of photographers around San Francisco who would soon break away from their studios to make landscape photographs and be financially rewarded for doing so. Glass plates ushered in the era of easy replicability, a necessity if photographers were to sell multiple copies of their most successful subjects.

San Francisco was the most important training ground in the United States for outdoor photographers at the crucial turning point in the mid-fifties when the daguerreotype died and the glass processes were entering a transition that changed the ground rules of photography. Robert Vance, one of the most successful San Francisco daguerreians, saw the direction of the future and obtained glass-plate equipment which C. L. Weed used to make photographs of the American River and Yosemite Valley in 1859 (Fig. 40). Weed's was a pioneering venture at photographing scenery for its own sake.[32] Carleton E. Watkins also probably learned glass-plate photography in Vance's studio about this time, although no photographs from his hand are recorded before 1861. By the mid-sixties Weed and Watkins would find themselves in heated competition, a competition from which Watkins emerged with a national reputation as a landscape photographer to whom even Albert Bierstadt would look as a model (Fig. 85).

38. Alonzo Chappel. Drawing after daguerreotype by J. Wesley Jones. Great Carson Cañon. CHS

40. C. L. Weed. The Yo Semite Fall, 2500 Ft. 1859. S. MMA

39. Broadside for "Jones's Great Pantoscope of California." About 1851. CHS

Photographers in Yosemite,

1861-1868

The chain of events surrounding the death of the daguerreotype and the birth of outdoor glass-plate photography in the Bay Area is not clear. Names of some of those who made important contributions have been lost, and the chronology of the development is sketchy.[33] Such important works as Watkins's breakaway Yosemite photographs of 1861 do not happen by chance, and it is unlikely that Watkins could have arrived at such an accomplishment without being directed by significant outside influences. Unfortunately, nothing substantial is recorded about Watkins's life between 1856 and 1860, when formative influences would have been strongest.

Photography went hand in hand with painting to effect the rise of landscape art on the West Coast; in the East the first landscape photographers had imitated the earlier work of painters. The first school of California landscape painting was established during the very years Watkins was emerging as a photographer of landscape. B. P. Avery notes in his 1868 art-historical survey of California that "the year 1862 began a period of more activity and promise for art on the Pacific . . . notable in the modest Art Annals of San Francisco for the first appearance of a number of landscape painters."[34] Avery's article chronicles the rise of landscape art in northern California and observes that before 1857 artists had confined themselves largely to portraiture; the first exhibition containing a num-ber of landscape paintings was in 1858, presenting the work of a half-dozen figures, among whom only F. A. Butman gained Avery's approval. Avery describes Butman as the first serious landscape artist in the state. He introduced the practice of making open-air studies which were later refined in the studio. Butman was his most popular between 1860 and 1865, at exactly the time Watkins and C. L. Weed were working. In 1865 an art museum, the California Art Union (Fig. 41), was established to exhibit the work of local artists as well as paintings by eastern landscape artists like Durand, Church, Bierstadt, Cropsey, Hart, Richard, Gifford, Johnson, Moran, and others.[35]

Watkins's landscape photographs were the earliest and most important examples of photography paralleling painting in the West. His work is significant since it occurred when most of his contemporaries were photographing other subjects. Watkins's work is further significant since a body of his photographs datable to 1861 exists to define his personal style. As a result of the anonymous way retailers such as the firm of Lawrence and House-worth (Fig. 42) labeled their photographs, the identities of other early photographers is obscured. Muybridge, for example, did not enter photographs for copyright until 1868 (Fig. 113); by then his work was sufficiently mature to suggest that he had been active earlier. The early sixties are nonetheless better documented than the infant years of glass-

41. Lawrence and Houseworth. California Art Union, Montgomery Street, from Eureka Theater. No. 147. About 1864. S. MMA

plate photography, between 1855–1860, simply because many more actual photographs are extant to which authorship can be attributed once the mature styles of the photographers have been determined.

Lawrence and Houseworth were authorized to sell photographs published with their imprint, the first of which was copyrighted in 1865. The firm purchased photographs from the handful of working professional photographers in the area, including Weed, Watkins, Hart, and Muybridge, but they sold primarily stereoscopic photographs obtained from publishers all over. E. and H. T. Anthony[36] of New York were the most important publishers of photographs in America at midcentury, and it appears that C. L. Weed, who first visited Yosemite with a camera in 1859, had his negatives printed by Anthony in 1860. The Weed photographs (Fig. 40) were quite primitive compared to Watkins's work of a year later and doubtless gave Watkins the incentive to make his own mammoth-plate views, the likes of which had never been seen before. Watkins was very adventuresome in striking out on his own to become a photographer-publisher; his initiative saved him from the anonymity into which some others of his generation fell. Neither Anthony nor his competitors at the New York Stereoscopic Company nor less ambitious enterprises, such as Cremer in Philadelphia and Bates in Boston nor even the prestigious London Stereoscopic Company of New York gave credit to the many photographers whose services made a wide variety of views available. It is not surprising that in San Francisco Lawrence and Houseworth and its successor, Thomas Houseworth and Company, did not credit their photographers either. The firm advertised itself as opticians, the occupation also followed by other pioneer publishers of photographs. Except for Watkins's photographs, the earliest of which are datable to 1861, the history of glass-plate outdoor photography in San Francisco is scanty until 1865, when Lawrence and Houseworth entered a large group of San Francisco views for

copyright, and 1866, when they entered a group of Yosemite views, the first published on the West Coast.

The authorship of those photographs is a very provocative question, because in 1867, about the time Thomas Houseworth became sole proprietor of the firm, a group of photographs was sent in his name to the jurors of the Paris International Exposition. Those were noted in the *Illustrated London News* of 14 September 1867, and the following June a bronze medal was awarded to Thomas Houseworth by the French consul in San Francisco, an event reported in the San Francisco *Bulletin* and subsequently reiterated in the 1869 edition of Houseworth's catalogue.[37] The award was decisive for the future course of photography in California because it specifically honored landscape and gave a direction to photography in the West.

While there is no doubt that Watkins's 1861 mammoth-plate and stereoscopic views established the standard by which all photographs of California landscape were measured, it is of more than academic interest to know whose views were actually seen by the jurors in Paris and given such unstinting praise. Logic suggests it must have been Watkins's views, but evidence points otherwise. The author of the photographs Houseworth sent to Paris was probably C. L. Weed, who made a great many of the photographs published with Houseworth's imprint during the sixties. Weed was never credited on the mounts and never sought to establish a public identity for himself as Watkins, Muybridge, and Hart did after 1867 and as Vance, Jones, and Fardon had done a decade earlier. Weed's never issuing photographs with his own imprint suggests that his livelihood came as a

42. Exterior of Lawrence and Houseworth's store, San Francisco. No. 169. 1864. s. LL

169. Exterior of Lawrence & Houseworth's Store,
317 and 319 Montgomery street, San Francisco.

43. C. L. Weed. El Capitan, 3,600 Feet High. 1865. M. NYPL

44. C. E. Watkins. El Capitan, 3,600 ft. Before 1866. M. NYPL

45. E. J. Muybridge. Tu-toch-ah-nu-lah, (Great Chief of the Valley). The Captain, 3,500 feet above Valley. 1867. H. UCB

camera operator for someone else. He did however, sign a limited number of prints in pencil.[38] Many of these are identical to mammoth-plate photographs on mounts with the imprint of Thomas Houseworth, evidence that Weed operated the mammoth camera for Houseworth, who, judging from the long period of time they remained in print, retained control of the negatives.[39] It is conceivable that Weed was the author of the San Francisco views entered by Lawrence and Houseworth for copyright in 1865. They were competent

if rather dry and suggest the styles of the prior decade. Weed had been to Yosemite in 1859, but his naïve sense of landscape suggests that the bulk of his experience had been in other kinds of photography.

Weed made his first mammoth-plate Yosemite views between Watkins's 1861 and 1866 work, probably in the summer of 1865. The estimated dating is based on two interesting pieces of circumstantial evidence: the dead tree still standing in his El Capitan (Fig. 43) and a branch still in place mid-

way up the scrawny pine in his Valley seen from the Mariposa Trail (Fig. 46). In Watkins's views from the same points the dead tree has fallen (Fig. 44), and the branch is missing (Fig. 47). The changes suggest that at least a full season had elapsed between the time of Weed's mammoth plates and Watkins's of 1866. Houseworth entered a large series of Yosemite stereographs for copyright in 1866, which further suggests that photographers working for him were active in Yosemite before that date. The question remains why Wat-

36

kins, the superior artist, would follow Weed and so directly compete with him. Weed's mammoth-plate views of Yosemite are flawed in ways that might seem minor today but which were very important to the nineteenth-century clientele. Weed appears to not have been experienced at coating the mammoth plate, since the collodion is often streaked, a fault Watkins overcame after his first Yosemite season, when even his small stereos were flawed. Weed must also have been inexperienced at making landscapes in 1865; he violated some of the most elementary esthetic principles of wet-plate landscape photography, the first rule of which was to depict trees without a trace of blur. That feat took immense patience, cunning, and experience at a time when exposures could take up to an hour in early morning or late afternoon light, a length of time Watkins is said to have regularly required.[40] E. L. Wilson emphasizes the desirability of motionless trees in his writing on Watkins's Yosemite photographs.[41] Moreover, Weed did not always exercise pristine taste in composing his photographs, nor did he show the most faultless judgment when he posed figures whose breezy postures sometimes detracted from the seriousness of the general subject (Fig. 46).

Eadweard Muybridge perhaps worked with Weed in Yosemite in the summer of 1865, which would have been very soon after Muybridge returned to California from England to commence his new career as a photographer. An association between the two is suggested by the mammoth-plate portrait of Muybridge seated awkwardly beneath the U.S. Grant sequoia (Fig. 48) on a tin box bearing Houseworth's name and looking as though he had been told to "go sit." The photograph appears in Houseworth's mount but, typically, has no other indication of authorship, which has led to the suggestion that it is a self-portrait. The pose and composition lack the subtlety that marks Muybridge's better-known work of 1867–1872, in which figures are consistently integrated into the setting rather than imposed upon it. Even when Muybridge occasionally appears in his own photographs, he subordinates himself nearly to the role of innocent bystander. Moreover, as a self-portrait the Grant sequoia photograph would have revealed a vanity unparalleled in the annals of mammoth-plate landscape photography. In his 1872 mammoth plates of Yosemite Muybridge included figures in the English manner, as tastefully placed compositional elements. His contemporaries doing mammoth-plate work, Watkins and Jackson, also never photographed themselves in a manner approaching portraiture. A fine example of a well-placed figure in an otherwise pure landscape photograph is Watkins's portrait of Galen Clark, the Keeper of the Big Trees, beneath one of the forest giants in his care (Fig. 49). The photograph of Muybridge bears all the characteristics of Weed's style as it is known through the New York Public Library portfolio of his work.

Muybridge's first signed landscape photographs are a group entered for copyright in 1868 (Pls. 65–69); they are characterized by the carefully chosen points of view, brilliant light effects, and certain geographical motifs not photographed before. Could Muybridge have been so successful without some prior experience in the valley? Watkins's photographs matured tremendously on visits after 1861, and Weed's first mammoth plates were certainly not triumphs. The experience of other photographers suggests that Muybridge, too, must have been in Yosemite before he made his professional debut in 1868. Certain of the mammoth-plate views published by Houseworth can be attributed to Muybridge on the basis of their cloud-filled skies and stop-motion water, effects possible between 1868 and 1870 (Fig. 50).

If Weed is the author of at least some of the prize-winning landscapes sent to Paris in 1867, the award to Houseworth would have disturbed other photographers around San Francisco. Watkins would have been incensed because it was he, after all, whose mammoth-plate photographs were famous not just in California, but also in the East where they were exhibited in New York's prestigious Goupil Gallery;[42] and it was he who had most methodically cultivated Yosemite as a motif.

It is conceivable that Houseworth even included some of Watkins's photographs in the group sent to Paris, for the description in the *Illustrated London News* evokes Watkins's work over Weed's. Indeed, the review notes several telling characteristics of Watkins's hand: that the photographs portrayed "most admirably the grand rock and river scenery of the country, which seems to abound with charming waterfalls, rapid rivers, and rocks with almost perpendicular faces rising 3,000 feet from their base," effects at the heart of Watkins's

48. Attributed to C. L. Weed. Eadweard Muybridge below the U.S. Grant sequoia. Published by Thomas Houseworth and Co. About 1865. M. SW

49. C. E. Watkins. Section of the "Grizzly Giant," 33 Feet Diameter, Mariposa Grove, Cal. No. 113. Published by I. Taber. 1866. M. MMA

vision of the landscape and features of his work as early as 1861. The notice also observes a subtle but important detail: "In none of these pictures do we see the least signs of man; not a log hut nor an ax-felled tree to indicate his presence: all seems wild, primitive nature, which gives the great charm to these excellent photographs."[43] Weed was fond of including people, and Watkins must surely be the subject of the London critic's remarks. The contrast between the two men's styles is nowhere more apparent than in Watkins's Yosemite Valley from the "Best General View" (1866) (Fig. 47) as seen with Weed's photograph of 1865/1866 from the same site (Fig. 46).

After the Houseworth medal, every photographer in California was well aware of the international hunger for photographs of raw landscape, and each had to question his own ability to produce such. Most marketed views of the mines or the towns and the people in them; they must have realized with some solemnity that what attracted the Europeans was the "grand rock and river scenery of the country . . . the charming waterfalls, rapid rivers, and rocks with almost perpendicular faces."[44] The result was for the serious working photographers to claim their share of Houseworth's fame. The earliest Watkins views are copyrighted 1867, the year Houseworth received his bronze medal. Watkins's first response to the applause unwittingly given to his work had been to sign his name and put negative numbers on his views. Immediately thereafter he would have mounts printed with his name and the copyright so there would be absolutely no mistaking the author of his glorious landscapes. The Paris award very likely caused Watkins to completely rethink the marketing of his work; he established his own studio and "Yosemite Art Gallery" in 1867 and arranged for Hardy Gillard to be his sole agent. Their relationship must have been short-lived and unsuccessful, as scarcely any of Watkins's photographs with Gillard's imprint are extant. Watkins was motivated to make other dramatic gestures in 1867.

50. Attributed to E. J. Muybridge. Tocoyae and Tissayack, North Dome, 3,725 ft. Published by Thomas Houseworth and Co. 1868–1870. M. IMP/GEH

51. E. J. Muybridge. The Lyell Group and Yosemite Falls from Sentinel Dome. About 1867. H. UCB

He sent a roll of his own mammoth-plate and stereo Yosemite views to the jurors of the Paris International Exposition, which had apparently continued for another year. The jury responded by awarding Watkins "the only medal for California views in 1868,"[45] a curious designation since Houseworth's medal was presented by the consul in June of 1868. In 1867 Watkins had stereo mounts printed up with his name and address and the number and title of each view; his numbering suggests that by 1867 he had made about fifteen hundred negatives,

which he then entered for copyright. In 1868 the verso of his card mount was imprinted with a design by his painter friend Thomas Keith. The motif is in exact imitation of the back of Houseworth's card declaring himself the proud winner of the prize for landscape.

The accolades heaped on California landscape photography in 1867 and 1868 caused a revolution in the Bay Area. Competition between Weed and Watkins raged as landscape became the subject of the moment. Both men photographed Yosemite

Valley from Inspiration Point, Weed deliberately posing a man near the tree and a woman near the rim (Fig. 46). But his framing of the view and choice of light is much less satisfactory than in Watkins's view, with its dynamic, if not unorthodox, composition with the truncated tree (Fig. 47). Moreover, Watkins's choice of light elegantly models the valley walls at the left, and his choice of a slightly different point of view shows Yosemite Falls to much better advantage. Similarly, it appears that in 1865 Weed made the view of El Capitan reflected in Mirror Lake prior to Watkins, whose 1866 view bests Weed's by capturing the lake in perfect stillness. The photographic duel ended in Watkins's favor. Each instance in which Watkins set his camera on the identical spot as Weed resulted in an image superior in composition or technique. Watkins, indeed, was to prove he was the master photographer of Yosemite, until Muybridge's work of 1872 seriously challenged his.

California landscape photography would continue to flourish in an intensely competitive environment. In 1868 Muybridge copyrighted a series of Yosemite views small in size (five and one-half-by eight and one-half-inch negatives) in which he attempted to distinguish his own photographs from the work of Watkins and Weed. Muybridge's entry onto the scene posed an additional competitive element for Watkins. Muybridge occasionally set up his camera at the identical spot as his two predecessors, as in the Lyell Group from Sentinel Dome (Figs. 51, 52), which suggests his obligation to those who preceded him. More often he attempted to distinguish himself by choosing dramatic points of view which had never before been seen in Yosemite photographs. He constantly sought viewpoints that enhanced the drama of a site and placed his work very much in contrast to Watkins's stoic frontal views.

Muybridge's Yosemite photographs—both those entered for copyright in 1868 (Pls. 65–69) and in 1873 (Pls. 70–83, 86, 87) were judged esthetically more successful than Watkins's parallel body of work, but the evaluation fails to consider that by 1867 Muybridge and Watkins were working from substantially different artistic premises. Muybridge was very much the mannered romanticist,[46] while Watkins was the essential classicist, eschewing visual gimmickry and opting to express as directly as possible his profound experience of nature. Muybridge attempted to photograph the drama of the Sierra Nevada, while Watkins probed its quietude; Muybridge sought to depict the visible forces at work in nature, while Watkins suggested the invisible ones so well articulated in prose by Louis Agassiz and Clarence King. Muybridge avoided formal, hieratic order whenever doing so intensified the drama of a picture and chose subjects to emphasize extremes of space, shape, and distance. Watkins, on the other hand, set about to reveal nature's harmony and to make portraits of its grandest features; the underlying artistic premise was truth rather than effect. Watkins sought to portray Yosemite and the surrounding area as a microcosm where universal harmony and calm prevailed among the elements, from the smallest rock or flower to the dominating face of El Capitan; each item existed as a necessary part of a perfectly orchestrated whole. Watkins idealized nature, treating it as the embodiment of a divine perfection, while for Muybridge nature was a series of juxtaposed paradoxes.

Watkins's and Muybridge's styles continued to balance and to set the pace for other landscape photographers between 1868 and 1873 in San Francisco. That city became the acknowledged capital of mammoth-plate photography, rivaled only by the later work of W. H. Jackson in Denver. The galleries of Houseworth, Watkins, and Bradley and Rulofson were meccas for photographers passing through. The influence they exerted on O'Sullivan, Russell, and others is difficult to measure, but Jackson unequivocally expressed his homage in a series of mammoth-plate photographs made in Yosemite after 1880.[47]

52. C. E. Watkins. The Lyell Group, 13,191 feet above sea and Nevada Fall from Sentinel Dome. No. 96. Published by I. Taber. 1866. M. MMA

Western Railroads and the Landscape of Travel

andscape consciousness in the 1860s was elevated in part by the pervasive art, literature, and writing on natural history and by the social and philosophical conclusions that followed. It was also fueled by a more practical series of developments after the completion of the western half of the transcontinental railroad (Fig. 53). The railroad linking Omaha to San Francisco was the primary force behind the burst of outdoor photography that took place in the wake of the Civil War and brought photographers in touch with land in a manner not too different from the war itself.[48] War photographers were engaged in photographing distinctive subjects—the dead on battlefields, fortifications, armaments, bridges, transportation vehicles, etc.—all of which rested in a landscape environment. Similarly, the railroads, as they penetrated to the Great Plains and the far West, became increasingly minute specks in a vast landscape. The photographers, while still concentrating on the essential subjects of tracks, locomotives, trestles, and water towers, were increasingly required to contend with the relationship between landscape and the immediate subject (Fig. 54).

The advent of the railroads prompted two types of landscape consciousness that bear on photography between 1862 and 1870. Photographers who were associated with the railroads during the construction phase, generally easterners, were seeing the immense scope of the plains and Rockies for the first time. They were asked to satisfy the needs of the railroad companies for photographs illustrating the progress of construction, and in their work landscape became the background. Among the railroad-hired easterners were A. J. Russell and Alexander Gardner, employed by the Union

53. A. J. Russell. Driving of the Golden Spike, Promontory, Utah, 10 May 1869. I. YU

54. John Carbutt. Westward the Monarch, Capitol Makes Its Way. 1866. s. LC

along the western railroads had the task of supplying views of landmarks which were sometimes as unpicturesque as the "Thousand Mile Tree" (Fig. 55) or of rock formations such as "Finger Rock," which were discovered by photographers.

The first phases of railroad construction were begun in California by the Central Pacific Railroad as early as 1861, when American landscape photography was still in its infancy. Consequently, the construction of the first sixty miles of track between Sacramento and the foothills of the Sierra Nevada during 1863–1865 are sparsely documented. The crescendo of activity in both West and East came after the war, between 1866 and 1869, when the summit of the Sierra Nevada at Donner Pass was achieved by the Central Pacific Railroad and the great distance between Omaha and Promontory, Utah, was realized by the workmen of the Union Pacific Railroad, who lay up to five hundred fifty-five miles of track in a single year.[49]

The financing of the Union Pacific Railroad was accomplished in a very imaginative manner by the

55. C. R. Savage. The Thousand Mile Tree. About 1869. s. MMA

56. John Carbutt. The Hundredth Meridian Excusion party on Pine Bluff. 1866. s. MMA

Pacific. Most other photographers were not employees of the railroads but rather worked independently making photographs on speculation for the expected stream of travelers who would, hopefully, want photographs as mementos. Entrepreneurial photographers began their work during the final stages of construction in 1868 and 1869. The first wave of speculative photographers included A. A. Hart, W. H. Jackson, and C. R. Savage as well as Watkins and Muybridge.

The speculators had no visual precedents, since they were delineating regions that had previously been entered only rarely. In contrast, when Frederick Langenheim photographed along the route of the Reading, Williamsport, and Elmira Railroad in 1855, his eye was guided by a decade of views by artists working in lithography, whose chosen subjects had become standard motifs by the time of his arrival. The first generation of photographers

vice-president, T. C. Durant. The photographer John Carbutt accompanied an excursion of "two hundred and fifty of the most distinguished citizens of America, two brass bands, reporters from practically every important newspaper in the country, a staff of chefs, a French marquis, an English earl, government commissioners, and Union Pacific Directors."[50] Carbutt made about three hundred stereoscopic photographs, many of which were of the excursionists and their social activities (Fig. 56). A substantial number of his photographs were of eccentric rock forms and other landscape features, such as Pine Bluff, with the excursionists dotted like ants around it, a composition that suggests the great pleasure the men took in the land itself. The photograph further conveys a suggestion of the qualities H. T. Williams in his early guidebook, *The Pacific Tourist*, described as "the blankness of desolation, the majesty of loneliness."[51]

It was perhaps difficult for eastern photographers to admire the desolation in the plains and Rockies because there were so many interesting active subjects—Indians, buffalo, Mormon emigrants (Fig. 57), and the military outfits—all of which presented attractive motifs that photographers like Ridgeway Glover went West particularly to photograph. They were motifs, however, that resisted treatment in photographs because the process was so slow. Glover, a young Philadelphia photographer, went to capture those motifs as special correspondent for *Leslie's Illustrated Weekly Magazine.* He was among the first Americans to exploit the instantaneous capacity of the negative-on-glass process, one of the features which made it so superior to the daguerreotype. Glover left his old negatives, including animal portraits and general outdoor work, in the care of the publishers Wenderoth and Taylor in Philadelphia in hopes that the sale of prints would help generate revenue to support his western journey. His letters reveal the subjects

that enchanted him and the difficulty of the conditions under which he worked. He said he photographed the Indians in Fort Laramie late in June 1866. As he proceeded farther West he wrote, "I am surrounded by beautiful scenery, and hemmed in by yelling savages."[52] By late August he wrote that he was very taken by the scenery but that he had not been able to secure many good negatives. Shortly afterward Glover was found scalped on the prairie, a demise which elevated him to martyrdom among adventuresome outdoor workers who longed to set out on their own.

Events such as the mock Indian attack staged by the U.P.R.R. for the One-hundredth Meridian Excursion party tend to give the idea that the region west of the Mississippi was tamed in 1866, but the Glover incident reveals that things were not really in as much control as they appeared. Glover was among the few independent photographers; the more usual course was for a photographer to attach himself to a formally organized party, such as

Carbutt or W. H. Illingworth did. Illingworth, a landscape photographer from St. Paul, accompanied the expedition of Capt. Fisk, who was blazing an overland route to the gold fields of Montana in 1866 (Fig. 58). On seeing Illingworth's views, Edward L. Wilson remarked that they "give one a fine idea of the tediousness, the loneliness, and the danger of a trip across the vast plains of the west ... there is but little to love in them."[53] Wilson might have seen little to love in the landscape of Montana, but Illingworth was a devoted landscape photographer and was among the small handful able to photograph nature with great compassion while constantly on the move.

A. J. Russell, also a former Civil War photographer (Fig. 173), specialized in photographs of the military railroad system and was a natural choice by the U.P.R.R. as the official photographer for the Western Division in 1868.[54] Russell's sensitivity to landscape and nature would not have been expected from one fresh from the war. He had a

57. Lawrence and Houseworth, publishers. Camp of Mormons at Lake Tahoe. About 1865. s. p

58. Illingworth and Bill. Camp at White Bear Den, Dakota Territory. 1866. s. p

59.
A. J. Russell. The Wind
Mill at Laramie. 1867/
1868. I. YU

developed sense of order and form in nature which enabled him to previsualize his photographs into strong compositions, such as the windmill at Laramie (Fig. 59), a monumental sculptural form rising from a scene of man-made chaos.

Russell avoided obvious visual solutions in his pursuit of the threefold theme of man, machine, and nature. His view of the new and old trestle near Citadel Rock on the Green River (Pl. 95) reveals the subtle balance he could achieve between the three elements. The snow-covered landscape is carefully punctuated with figures posed with the delicacy of a formal portrait. Russell might have set up his camera between the two sets of tracks. The result is a finely realized balance in scale and position between the people, the bluff, and the locomotive. But no matter how carefully staged the photograph is, the snow-dusted elegance of the

rock formation makes the work of man look clumsy and temporary.

Russell pursued the theme of nature's prevalence over man and his works in many photographs, of which his view of Hanging Rock, Foot of Echo Canyon (Pl. 90) in Utah is the most dramatic example. Russell brilliantly created the illusion that the buildings and the man would be crushed by the slightest movement of the formation; he played the role of the grand dramatist imposing an interpretation that would not be repeated in the hundreds of photographs of Hanging Rock made after 1869, when it became one of the favorite sites of cross-country travelers.

Russell's photograph of High Bluff, Black Buttes (Pl. 98) and his Skull Rock (Pl. 91) use the presence of figures to foster an illusion and a heightened sense of drama. High Bluff is not very high

at all, but Russell suggests a dangerous feat of mountaineering by depicting a human chain leading to the pinnacle. Skull Rock introduces an element of irony approaching humor in the figure swaggeringly astride the top.

Certain of Russell's photographs, like Granite Canyon from the Water Tank (Pl. 92) and Malloy's Cut (Pl. 89), contain figures merely for scale rather than for drama or illusion. Both are incredibly direct, simply conceived photographs, in which staging for dramatic intensity is at a minimum. In Granite Canyon the two figures are posed with sublime perfection as symbols of the human role in laying tracks across twenty-two hundred miles. Moreover, the photograph suggests, in the crooked track and the crudely shaped ties, that if this is a work of sophisticated engineering genius, the genius lies with whoever moved the earth and set the grade.

Russell was a superb photographic journalist, a master of the devices with which a photograph can be made interesting: by the addition of figures and by subtle adjustments in the composition and by repeating visual themes to give the photographs narrative continuity. He did not exhibit the nearly religious love of nature that Watkins showed, nor did he have the very subtle narrative and compositional sensibility of Hart or Muybridge's diversity of subjects. He is, nonetheless, the most interesting eastern photographer to rise through the patronage of the railroad.

Among the photographers who worked not as employees of the railroads but as entrepreneurs making views for the imminent stream of westward travelers was A. A. Hart of Sacramento, who photographed along the route of the Central Pacific between Sacramento and Promontory, Utah. His work actually began during the construction, perhaps because the engineering problems surmounted by the genius of the chief engineer, T. D. Judah, were deemed of more lasting interest than were the expanses of track over the prairies and deserts that confronted Russell. Hart was a pho-

60. A. A. Hart. Alcove in Palisades, Ten Mile Cañon. No. 399. Published by C. E. Watkins. About 1868. s. MMA

tographer of great talent, whose mysterious death in 1869, at about the time of the driving of the Golden Spike, ended what would have certainly been a productive career in photography. Hart's vision of the railroad was addressed not so much to the glory of iron and steel as to the intrusion of man on nature.

His photograph of the Alcove in Palisades, Ten Mile Canyon (Fig. 60) is a perceptive commentary on the interaction of machine and nature, for here the iron horse becomes completely subordinated to the environment. The locomotive has just entered the frame of vision with most of the car omitted. The tracks looming in the right foreground will eventually bring the train face to face with the camera. Hart consistently chose his points of view so that the tracks played a significant, but sometimes understated, role in composition. His Forest View, near Dutch Flat (Fig. 61) shows but a thin sliver of track dramatically intersected by a gently sloping bank of earth, suggesting in a gentle way how minute human work is within the context of nature.

Esthetically Hart had much in common with C. E. Watkins. They shared a capacity to reveal the ultimate harmony in the world at large. Watkins addressed himself to the pure harmony of nature, while Hart expressed concordance rather than paradox in the relationship between industrial man and virgin nature. Hart's device was visual: the locomotive compared but subordinated to the rugged rock cliff in Alcove in Palisades and the tracks similarly understated in Forest View. Both photographs were designed to reveal essential qualities about both nature and the railroad. Watkins and Hart also shared the capacity to see trees, rocks, and valleys with a classical and harmonic sense of space and composition, in contrast to nature as chaotic and paradoxical in Muybridge's vision.

61. A. A. Hart. Central Pacific Railroad, Forest View, near Dutch Flat. No. 65. s. MMA

The esthetic kinship between Watkins and Hart was fortuitously sustained after Hart's early demise, when Watkins came into possession of Hart's three hundred sixty-odd glass plates and printed them over the years as his own.[55] The negatives Watkins had were all made between 1865 and 1869, judging from the advanced stages of the construction pictured. However, given Hart's sophisticated eye, he must have been photographing earlier. Watkins's ownership of the Hart negatives suggests that he thought enough of Hart's work to put his name to it. The esthetic similarities between the two men's work suggests there was more than a routine business arrangement between them; it is possible that Watkins was acquainted with Hart during his lifetime, as is tantalizingly suggested by Hart's photograph of Stumps Cut by Donner Party in 1846.[56] The picture contains a prominently posed man dressed in a photographer's smock who bears a remarkable resemblance to Watkins's lean and bearded figure. Whether or not Watkins and Hart were actually acquainted, it is not inconceivable that each saw the other's photographs and that Watkins's love of pure landscape influenced Hart's work, or vice versa.

Like Hart, C. R. Savage of Salt Lake City was drawn to photographing landscape as an outgrowth of his railroad activity, although other circumstances caused him to be more directly involved with pure landscape. Savage had made a journey of nearly nine thousand miles to the East and back in 1866 to purchase supplies, including a wagon outfitted as a darkroom. He had the merchandise shipped by train to Nebraska City, and from there he proceeded to Salt Lake City in the company of a Mormon emigrant train.[57]

Savage was British, and his photographs represent a head-on confrontation between the visual language of European picturesque romanticism and the reality of cactus and sagebrush in the des-

CENTRAL PACIFIC RAILROAD.
Illustrated by C. R. Savage.

CENTRAL PACIFIC RAILROAD.
Illustrated by C. R. Savage.

ert of the Great Basin. He saw in the bleak landscape of Utah some of the qualities Francis Frith (Fig. 21) perceived in the Sinai. The Sink of the Humboldt (Fig. 62) takes on the appearance of the River Jordan and the Temples of the Rio Virgen (Fig. 63) become like Mount Horeb. Savage greatly admired Watkins's work, and his own landscape is a perfect gradation from sand and stone, through sagebrush and boulder, to the main subject, in the distance, as an expression of the harmony of raw nature.

W. H. Jackson's earliest sustained effort photographing under expeditionary circumstances, and his first landscape work, occurred on a speculative trip along the Union Pacific Railroad (Figs. 179–181, 183) between Omaha and Salt Lake City after the railroad opened in 1869. Jackson's diaries[58] reveal the process of his gaining experience in out-

63. C. R. Savage. Temples of the Rio Virgen (Utah). About 1870. s. MMA

62. C. R. Savage. Sink of the Humboldt (Utah?). About 1870. s. MMA

UTAH.
Illustrated by C. R. Savage.

UTAH.
Illustrated by C. R. Savage.

Temples of the Rio Virgin.

door photography at a time when he was still seeking to define his artistic personality. He photographed the obvious natural monuments along the railroad route, many times including figures in artificial poses (Fig. 64). Jackson did not explore the sculptural qualities of the rock formations but rather chose frontal points of view that reduced the forms to two-dimensional designs. His stereographs of 1869 perversely deny the stereoscopic rendering of volume.

Jackson's diary records his having seen Russell's negatives in Echo, Utah, and the influence of the more experienced photographer's work can be seen in Jackson's photograph of Skull Rock, which is a pastiche of Russell's photograph of a year earlier (Pl. 91).[59]

Russell had considerable influence on other photographers as well, for even the seasoned C. R. Savage was indebted to Russell's Hanging Rock, but Savage's version was taken after the telegraph lines had been erected and after an addition to the frame house below was made. Photographers, like visual artists in other media, sought models for their work, and it was to Russell's credit that he was imitated.

It took energy and imagination for photographers to envision pictures that travelers might want to purchase. Moreover, the example of Jackson's early work suggests how reluctant nature was to reveal its form and structure to those inexperienced at seeing it.

Government Patronage

The year 1867 was a turning point in the history of American landscape photography, when a new force propelled photographers into contact with the land. Clarence King's Fortieth Parallel Survey was established by the United States Government, and an ambitious program of exploring, mapping (Fig. 65), and studying the far West ensued. It was a program that brought photographers in touch with the land in a way that profoundly influenced the future of landscape photography.[60] Before 1867 photographers were motivated to some degree by the requirements of making a living from their profession alone, as clearly described in W. H. Jackson's diaries of 1869.[61] However, the commerce in outdoor photographs was so meager prior to 1870 that it did not easily yield a livelihood. Indeed, outdoor photographers had almost no models, and few, if any,

except C. E. Watkins based their reputations on the photography of pure landscape before 1865.

Watkins was the first photographer to serve with the post-Civil War geographical and geological survey parties. He was in Yosemite in the summer of 1866, coincidentally, at the same time as Josiah D. Whitney with his crew from the California State Geological Survey. Whitney's mission, made at the request of the Commissioners to Manage the Yosemite Valley, was to measure the region after it was declared a public pleasure area by the Congress in 1864.[62] Whitney, doubtless familiar with Watkins's impressive mammoth-plate views and stereos of Yosemite from 1861, arranged for him to photograph for the survey. Watkins's participation is acknowledged in the early pages of the report prepared by Whitney, but Watkins must have been associated on an informal basis, since he

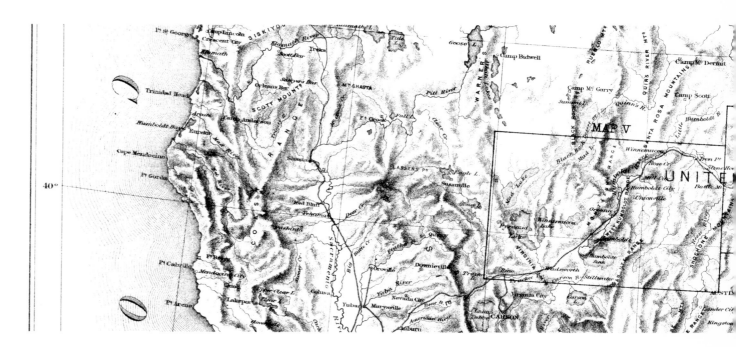

65. Detail of map of the Clarence King Survey of the regions along the fortieth parallel. 27½ x 21⅝ in. NA

made a great many negatives independently that summer. It must have been a very exciting time for Watkins, as he produced some of his most successful Yosemite photographs.

The Yosemite Book (1868), as Whitney called the report of the Yosemite survey, was the model for subsequent geological and geographical survey publications. It contained fifty of Watkins's original photographs and was published for the park commission by Julius Bien of New York in an edition of two hundred fifty copies. Copies were distributed to influential politicians and sold to the general public. Clarence King was one of Whitney's assistants that summer, as was James T. Gardner; both of them would soon be engaged in King's Fortieth Parallel Survey.

Watkins's 1866 photographs represent a significant stylistic evolution from his well-known earlier work. The points of view become more frontal (Figs. 44, 52, Pl. 14) and there is less concern for a picturesque balancing of major topographical features against minor ones. The evolution can be attributed to the specific competitive influence of Weed's 1865 series and to the outspoken esthetics of Clarence King. Watkins carried on a close visual dialogue with the survey, but he does not appear to have been on their payroll. He made simultaneous exposures with the survey's half-plate camera and his own mammoth-plate and stereo equipment. For that reason mammoth-plate views Watkins published on his own duplicate those published in smaller format in *The Yosemite Book*. The changes in Watkins's style are not dramatic enough to suggest he was asked to make geological illustrations but are rather the normal artistic progress based on already established working patterns. In this regard his role as a survey photographer is quite different from the working arrangements of O'Sullivan, Jackson, and E. O. Beaman, who were involved in active collaboration with geologists on other surveys. Watkins proved that artistic landscape photography was not distant from the goals of a survey and that the ends of pure landscape coincided to a great extent with the ends of pure geology and geography.

Clarence King's graduate education took place when he volunteered for the Whitney Survey in 1864; among the lessons he learned was the usefulness of photography to the geologist. Congress appropriated funds to establish the Geological Exploration of the Fortieth Parallel in 1867, and among the first appointments King made was that of Timothy O'Sullivan as photographer. It is not clear why King did not ask Watkins to join him,

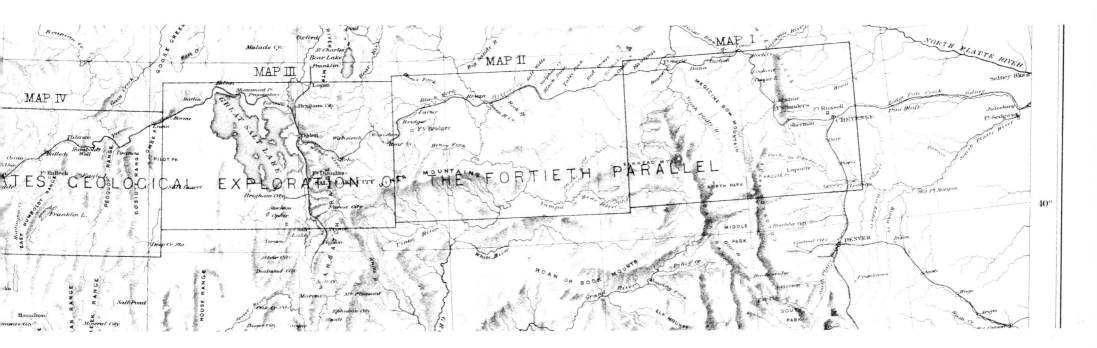

since he once said Watkins was the best photographer he knew.[63] Perhaps it was because in 1868 Watkins was on a trip to northern California and Oregon with the painter William Keith.[64] O'Sullivan was in Washington working for Alexander Gardner, and as an army photographer, would have been familiar to Gen. A. A. Humphreys, the commander of the Corps of Engineers, under which King's survey was operated.

King's use of O'Sullivan was in many ways a more important precedent than Watkins's work on the Whitney Survey. Whitney's Yosemite work lasted only two years and was mainly of local importance, but King set a very important example for the use of photography on the massive government surveys (Fig. 66). F. V. Hayden's Survey of the Territories was also formed in 1867, but he did not employ W. H. Jackson as photographer (Pls. 104–112) until 1870, after King had displayed O'Sullivan's photographs in Washington as an aid to his appropriation renewal in 1869.[65] John Wesley Powell first went down the Colorado River in 1869, but he did not hire a photographer until his second venture downriver in 1871, when he employed the talented eastern landscapist E. O. Beaman, who was replaced halfway through the season by Jack Hillers. Lt. George Wheeler inherited O'Sullivan from King for the first season's work on his Geographical Surveys West of the One Hundredth Meridian in 1871. King, meanwhile, had hired Watkins for the ascent of Mount Shasta.

King (Fig. 67) had spent 1863, the year following his graduation from Yale's Sheffield Scientific School, in New York on a kind of *wanderjahr*. While in the city he became fascinated by the writings of John Ruskin and joined the radical Ruskinians in New York, the Society for Truth in Art. Ruskin had great admiration for photographs, as they embodied many of the principles he valued in art; the Ruskinians saw in the photograph a medium capable of recording the minute aspects of nature, like the texture of granite or a forest thicket, which resisted treatment with brush or pencil.[66] King, like Hayden, had great respect for artists and was a dilettante himself. He collected paintings and befriended artists, and his interests matured in the year prior to his departure for the West; his love of the arts remained an influence on him for the rest of his life. Thus, when he arrived in San Francisco in 1867 to lead the Fortieth Parallel Survey, his head was filled with ideas far beyond the specifics of geology.

The patronge of photographers by the heads of surveys took many forms, the most significant of which was financial, but the esthetic contribution and the intellectual ambiance cannot be underestimated. For the first time photographers were subsidized and encouraged to make pictures of unusual, largely unsalable, subjects. O'Sullivan was first paid one hundred dollars a month by King, then Wheeler paid him one hundred fifty dollars,[67] a handsome salary equal to that of the younger scientists with college degrees. Room and board in the field and transportation to and from the East each season was supplied gratis by the survey. Those amenities were incentive enough to attract W. H. Jackson to volunteer his first season with Hayden, which immediately followed his tiring summer of 1869, when he wrung a living from photographing along the Union Pacific Railroad.

66. Colton's Map of California, Nevada, Utah, Colorado, Arizona and New Mexico. 1864. 25½ x 16 in. P

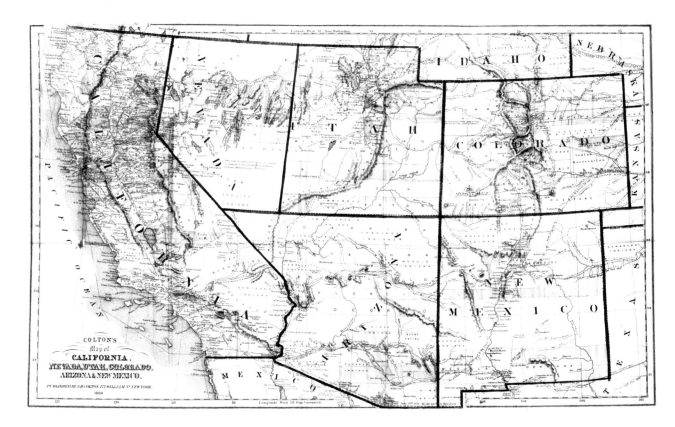

Survey life must have been luxurious by comparison.

Government photographers had a great advantage in terms of equipment. Photographers did not always own their cameras, which were generally supplied by the proprietor of studios to "operators," who actually made the photographs. This was the usual arrangement in portrait studios but was also common practice when Robert Vance supplied C. L. Weed with the wet-plate equipment he used along the American River before 1859. Muybridge is portrayed on a box bearing Houseworth's name (Fig. 48), and Houseworth unquestionably supplied a mammoth-plate camera that was used in Yosemite in 1864/1865 to make photographs with his studio imprint. However, California photographers took the lead in establishing themselves as independent outdoor artists; Muybridge had his own equipment by 1867.

Watkins was among the first landscape photographers in the United States to outfit himself for making every type of outdoor photograph. In addition to a stereoscopic camera he had a mammoth-plate camera, a piece of equipment not used on a government survey until W. H. Jackson used one on the Hayden Survey during the 1874 season. King was given permission to hire Watkins and his equipment for part of 1872 at a cost of three thousand dollars, which indicates the value of such an outfit.[68]

King and Wheeler supplied Timothy O'Sullivan with the equipment he used. After consultation with L. E. Walker, photographer to the Treasury Department, O'Sullivan listed the equipment he required for the King Survey and purchased it in 1867 from the firm of E. and H. T. Anthony in New York. King's records do not show his capital outlay, but when George Wheeler outfitted O'Sullivan in early 1871, a thousand dollars were spent on camera, lens, glass, and miscellaneous necessities, a price that was one-tenth the first-year appropriation for the entire survey.[69] O'Sullivan's equipment included a stereoscopic camera that made

67. A. J. Russell, on the mount of T. H. O'Sullivan. Taking Breath (Clarence King). 1869. F. NYPL

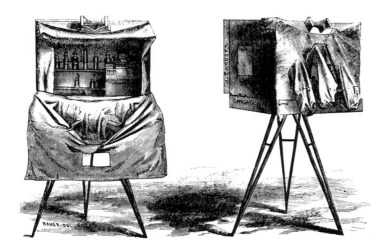

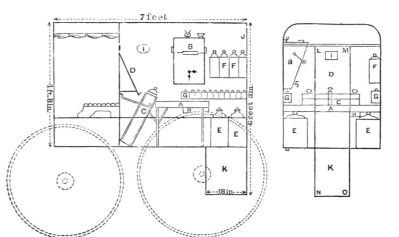

68. Carbutt's Portable Developing Box. Woodengraving in *The
Philadelphia Photographer*, January 1865. MMA

69. T. H. O'Sullivan. Detail of Carbutt's portable developing box
in use in Ruby Valley, Nevada. 1868. F. AGS

RIGHT:
71. C. E. Watkins. Salt Lake City from Arsenal Hill (with
Watkins's photographic van). About 1872. F(?). USHS

54

glass negatives of 5 by 8 inches and another camera that made 9½-by-11½-inch negatives. He used one of John Carbutt's patent developing boxes (Figs. 68, 69)[70] and transported it in a military ambulance that was apparently not as elegant as the photographic vans used by some of his contemporaries. George Rockwood's van (Fig. 70) had compartments and containers for the materials essential for outdoor photography in the East, but it was not suited to O'Sullivan's needs when he photographed at sites inaccessible to wheeled vehicles.

Bay Area photographers pioneered the use of photographic vans similar to Rockwood's. Watkins traveled to Utah with William Keith in such a van (Fig. 71), and Muybridge carted his materials around San Francisco in one. However, both men used European-style dark tents (Fig. 73) for their wilderness work, Muybridge calling his "The Flying Studio (Fig. 74)."

Income and equipment were important assets for the government photographers; King and Wheeler were deluged with applications for the coveted

72. C. R. Savage. Detail of photographic van in the desert. About 1870. s. MMA

73. European-style portable dark tent. Woodengraving in J. Thomson, ed., *A History and Handbook of Photography*, 1877. MMA

74. E. J. Muybridge ("Helios"). The Flying Studio. No. 114. 1872. s. LL

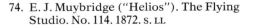

staff posts. Employment with the government was also a very good recommendation for future work. Muybridge widely published his few months' work with Gen. Halleck and touted himself on the Pacific Coast as the government photographer for the War and Treasury departments, a claim which is not supported by collections of extant photographs produced for those agencies.

One of the most important advantages of the survey work was the free service of assistants, who carried the many pounds of equipment (Fig. 75) required in wet-plate photography. Each party included skilled packers, whose job it was to get the mules loaded in the most efficient manner possible, an important consideration when a whole dark chamber had to be erected at each site. Moreover, many of the scientists were intrigued by photography and were generous to the favored photographers; J. T. Gardner, S. F. Emmons, W. H. Brewer, and G. K. Gilbert were among the most avid supporters of photography. Watkins, Jackson, O'Sullivan, and Bell each were accompanied by naturalists who often made note of the progress of photography in their letters and journals.[71]

Each of the great surveys was organized in a slightly different manner, but the general working procedure was for the full party–thirty to forty persons and a military escort—to assemble in a central location. Parties of three to ten men would then set out in separate directions to work specific areas and reconvene at the central point to restock supplies or begin a new foray. The photographer could accompany only one party at a time, and very often, as with O'Sullivan and Jackson, he would lead his own independent platoon. Those were luxurious circumstances; the choice of subject and the manner of presentation were the photographer's decisions alone.

75. W. H. Jackson. U.S. Geological Survey en route. 1871. F. ANS

Science, Nature, and Art

Science and art have been interconnected since the Renaissance, but their relationship has been obscured in the twentieth century. Photography was an art born of science, and the flowering of landscape photography was one expression of the ongoing interdependence between the two liberal arts: C. E. Watkins methodically made portraits of trees, identifying each by its proper Latin name as if to associate his handiwork with that of the scientist; his motivations in making the tree studies and in so naming them can only be guessed, but the photographs radiate his deep appreciation for the trees as objects (Pls. 32, 33; Fig. 86).

The interaction between Timothy O'Sullivan and the scientists on the King Survey resulted in a body of visual evidence and prolific writing that sheds considerable light on their working relationship. O'Sullivan was directed by both King and the geologist S. F. Emmons to make photographs that provided evidence for King's theory of "catastrophism" and Emmons's more sober principle of "mechanical geology"—an outgrowth of King's thinking. Catastrophism had deep socioreligious implications, indeed, was overtly anti-Darwinian in all its premises. King wanted to prove in his geology that sudden and violent changes occurred, which not only caused geological upheavals, but which had happened in recent enough history that the "experience of sudden, unusual telluric energy . . . [left] a terrible impression burned upon the very substance of human memory."[72] The most widely acknowledged theory of geology was uniformitarianism, propounded by Charles Lyell and refined by Darwin, which held that change in nature was gradual. King was adamantly opposed to the concept that man evolved from primates and hoped to prove by geological evidence that "if catastrophes extirpated all life at oft repeated intervals from the time of its earliest introduction, then creation must necessarily have been oft repeated."[73] King invoked the cosmogony of Sanskrit, Hebrew, and Islam as well as the Bible, which he quoted in a very fundamentalist way. King's position was a typical expression of his Unitarian background, which fostered the nature-oriented spiritualism that guided his life. He would now be considered very conservative scientifically, compared to a Darwinian like Harvard's Asa Gray, but in his time King's words and deeds had the ring of progress.

It is not surprising to find that O'Sullivan's photographs from 1867/1868 reflect an attempt to gather visual evidence for catastrophism, as did William Bell's photographs on the Wheeler Survey of 1872—on which Emmons was also working to gather evidence for his theory of mechanical geology. O'Sullivan photographed latent natural phenomena such as Geyser Mouth, Ruby Valley (Pl. 41), and Tufa Rocks, Pyramid Lake (Pl. 36). O'Sullivan's Geyser Mouth represented latent future change, while his Tufa Rocks of volcanic origin represented violent change in the near past, as did "Karnak," Montezuma Range, Nevada (Fig. 137). The photographs themselves are powerful images, almost iconic. They are not only evidence for King's geological theories but would also have pleased John Ruskin. They are compelling for their perfect points of view and describe better than drawings the accumulated details that ultimately compose rocks, trees, and mountains. Tufa Rocks and Volcanic Ridge (Pl. 37) are composed of small, perfectly formed shapes, the cumulative presence of which defines the character of the rocks. These were the very qualities valued by Ruskin when he said of drawing and painting, "It is just as impossible to generalize granite and slate as it is to generalize a man or a cow."[74]

76. Wm. Bell. Perched Rock, Rocker Creek, Arizona. 1872. F. BPL

77. Wm. Bell. The northern wall of the Grand Cañon of the Colorado, near the foot of the To-ro-weap Valley. No. 14. s. P

OPPOSITE PAGE, TOP:
78. Wm. Bell. The "Vermillion Cliff." No. 15. 1872. s. P

OPPOSITE PAGE, BOTTOM ROW:
79. Thomas Houseworth and Co., publishers. The Magic Tower—On the Union Point Trail. About 1867. s. MMA

80. C. E. Watkins. Agassiz Rock, near Union Point. No. 3149. 1874. s. MMA

81. E. J. Muybridge. Ten Pin Rock, Union Point. No. 1401. Published by Bradley and Rulofson. About 1872. s. MMA

William Bell photographed Perched Rock (Fig. 76) on the Wheeler expedition of 1872 when he was under the direction of G. K. Gilbert, one of the geologists employed by Wheeler. The rock stands like a piece of sculpture that might fit into either the traditional or modern esthetic. Moreover, the photograph is conceived with suggestive details; the figure is carefully placed to echo as a positive shape the negative curve of the rock's edge. An element of drama is introduced by the figure's placement below a precariously balanced rock whose presence, at least visually, tempts fate. Perched Rock is a beautiful image on many levels. Bell photographed the rock and other subjects (Figs. 77, 78) to illustrate Emmons's mechanical geology; O'Sullivan photographed Rock Carved by Drifting Sand for the same reason (Pl. 58).

Emmons was also on the Wheeler Survey (Pls. 56-64) after he left King's Fortieth Parallel Survey.

He proposed that all changes in the earth's surface take place through movement, which includes the movements of elevation and subsidence in the earth's surface, of volcanic flows, and of water. Perched Rock was dramatic evidence of movement caused by wind, a source of energy not anticipated in the original hypothesis.[75] Bell doubtless photographed the rock as evidence for the theory being pursued by several geologists at once. This does not mean that Bell visualized the rock any less intensely than if he had chosen it himself. Regardless of the reasons it was photographed, Perched Rock is a powerful natural icon that communicates on many different levels, as do all successful works of art.

Many photographers focused their attentions on the Agassiz Column between about 1870 and 1900, not solely because of its accessibility. They saw beauty in the formation, and it suggested a meaning beyond the literal. The series of photographs reveals much about the esthetic principles guiding landscape photography in the late nineteenth century.

The Agassiz Column was photographed, however insensitively, as early as about 1868 (Fig. 79) by an agent of the publisher Thomas Houseworth. C. E. Watkins photographed the rock in about 1870 (Pl. 26) and printed the first photographs bearing the name "Agassiz" in about 1875 (Fig. 80). A series of photographs by various photographers, including many views executed up until the turn of the century, demonstrate the powerful effect of the individual photographer's eye and imagination on the resulting image.

Watkins's two photographs of such a minimal motif as the column reveal how very differently a single artist can visualize his subject. In the photograph made about 1870 he delineated the granular structure of the granite and its evocative fissures by choosing a light that subtly modeled three intersecting planes. In the later photograph Watkins did an artistic about-face in creating a highly dramatic composition with strong contrasts of light and shadow, which exceeded Muybridge's (Fig. 81) visual pyrotechnics.

Watkins named the column for Louis Agassiz,

82. C. E. Watkins. Louis Agassiz. About 1870. CDV. HU

America's most prominent anti-Darwinian scientist, and to Watkins's mind the rock formation must have symbolically represented certain aspects of Agassiz's thought. Clarence King had attended Agassiz's popular lectures at Harvard in 1863—taking leave from Yale to do so—and was an outspoken admirer of his theories.[76] It is possible that Watkins himself heard Agassiz's lecture on the principles of natural history in San Francisco in 1870. King may even have introduced the two. However it happened, they did meet, and Watkins photographed the eminent teacher (Fig. 82); it is one of the few Watkins portraits extant.

King and his associates had introduced Watkins to the art of photographing rocks as still-life studies on Mount Lassen (Fig. 83) earlier in 1870, and the Agassiz Column was probably made soon afterward. The photograph begs for phallic interpretation; perhaps that effect is Watkins's attempt to demonstrate that the "relations and proportions which exist throughout the animal and vegetable world have an intellectual and ideal connection. . . ."[77] For Agassiz, the proof of the Creator was nature itself; the form, shape, and structure of nature were only symbols of Him. The harmony of natural forms was a manifestation of a divine and illimitable intellect.

Clarence King was not the first to bring the Universalist thought of Agassiz to San Francisco. He was preceded by an influential figure who coincidentally bore his surname—the Rev. Thomas Starr King. Starr King, a gifted preacher, left the famed Hollis Street Church in Boston for San Francisco, where he captivated his congregation. William H. Brewer, who first introduced Josiah Whitney and Clarence King to the virtues of photography for geologists, described King's sermon of 13 April 1862 as "a most brilliant and eloquent performance . . . the crowd in church could scarcely be restrained from bursting out with enthusiasm."[78]

Starr King also spoke of nature as a "vessel" full of spiritual meanings, a belief he articulated in his writings and lectures. He held that

. . . every gigantic fact in nature is the index and vesture of a gigantic force; everything which we call organization that spots the landscape of nature is a revelation of a secret force that has been wedded to matter. . . . Thus the stuff that we weigh, handle and tread upon is only the show of invisible substances, the facts over which subtle and mighty forces rule.[79]

Shortly after his arrival in San Francisco, Starr King had written a series of letters to the *Boston Globe* describing his 1860 visit to Yosemite with great emphasis on forms, textures, and colors. He concluded that "an artist who loves rocks might revel in it for a dozen life-times."[80] Starr King's account of his Yosemite experiences conceivably prompted Watkins's first trip there in 1861.

It appears that Watkins, like O'Sullivan and Bell, was deeply influenced by science, which was in turn influenced by philosophy and religion. All three men worked in a rare moment in the history of art when art and science were perfectly compatible.

It might seem that photographers merely illustrated the words and writings of articulate and educated eastern scientists. But it is doubtful that Watkins could ever have been told in any more than a very general way what to photograph. His character as it emerges from his survey photographs suggests aloofness and independence. While he might have listened to those around him, he spent a great deal of time intimately appreciating the works of nature. His prebankruptcy photographs have a deeply meditative quality that could not have been contrived.

O'Sullivan's working procedure is never described any more fully than Watkins's, but many more records exist from which it can be reconstructed. King's messianic enthusiasm would have affected everyone around him, but his presence was not absolute domination. While he doubtless suggested motifs to O'Sullivan, the photographer was free to locate them on his own. Indeed, O'Sullivan's own love for the land was apparent very early in his first season with King. The botanist

83. C. E. Watkins. North Side, Lassen's Peak. 1870.
I. IMP/GEH

W. W. Bailey recalled that O'Sullivan took the initiative in locating a rock outcropping of particular beauty (Fig. 18); Bailey and O'Sullivan together climbed a peak where they found a granite formation that appeared to have once been liquid blown by a breeze that solidified it.[81] Only O'Sullivan actually reached the site, where he made a photograph he called simply "Rock, Humboldt Mountains" and another view with the valley in the background (Fig. 84). O'Sullivan was clearly entranced by the landscape he was experiencing, even though it was like nothing he had seen before. He quickly developed a sense of the elementary beauty of the scrub plants, jagged hills, and strange formations that might have been overlooked by the casual walker.

Bailey described returning alone to the rock O'Sullivan had recorded and reveling in the "extreme solitude of the walk." His description has little to do with scientific observation and concludes with a note that "there was no live color on the scene, and yet it does not lack beauty." Bailey suggests that O'Sullivan was exhilarated by the land and that in initiating the excursion to Wave Rock he was demonstrably affected by the esthetics of his surroundings. Bailey himself described nature as if it were a work of art, and, conversely, O'Sullivan's photographs of 1868 are more than mere documents for a geological archive.[82] Had more extensive records been kept of the surveys Muybridge, Jackson, and Watkins accompanied, it would surely be found that their responses to the land were not significantly different from O'Sullivan's.

84. T. H. O'Sullivan. East Humboldt Mountains. About 1868. F. AGS

Photographers, Artists, and Critics

85. Albert Bierstadt (1830–1902). The Grizzly Giant. Oil on canvas. After 1864. 117 x 50 in. P

86. C. E. Watkins. The Grizzly Giant. Version A of three versions. Before 1864. I. P

One of the earliest historians of western landscape art, B. P. Avery, described photography in 1868 as "a handmaid of the fine arts, for the transcripts of scenery . . . which it furnishes are often valuable as guides and suggestors."[83] What Avery observed was a crucial factor in the development of photography: the interaction between photographer and artist.

The idea that photographs were useful aids to painting and drawing was not new. European painters like Delacroix had used daguerreotypes as models, and other artists, like Achille Devéria, were serious photographers themselves. In America Frederic Church assembled a large collection of photographs, which he consulted for his epic panoramas of South America.[84]

The painter Albert Bierstadt's brother Charles was a photographer, and Bierstadt himself had attempted to make photographs when he accompanied the F. W. Lander Expedition west in 1858/1859. Bierstadt's surviving photographs (Figs. 33, 34) have a primitive quality that suggests he was not successful in his earliest attempts and for that reason relied on the photographs of others. In the summer of 1864 on his first visit to Yosemite, Bierstadt based a painting of the Grizzly Giant (Fig. 85) on the photograph by Watkins (Fig. 86), even reproducing its perspectival distortions. Bierstadt painted other motifs in Yosemite Valley that echo Watkins's photographs, but none are based so directly on a single image as the Grizzly Giant. Bierstadt probably gained more than Watkins from their acquaintance; perhaps their artistic temperaments were too different for the kind of spontaneous exchange of ideas and images that took place between Bierstadt and Muybridge when both were in Yosemite in 1872.

By as early as 1867 Watkins had developed a longstanding friendship with the painter William Keith. In 1868 the two traveled to northern Califor-

87. C. E. Watkins. Thomas Hill's paintings in Lick House, San Francisco. About 1870. s. MMA

nia and Oregon together, and in December 1873 both went to Utah in Watkins's two-horse photographic van. Keith made no secret of using Watkins's photographs as models. Their friendship was supported by shared esthetics; both believed that nature required no embellishment and that the simplest, most straightforward rendering of natural motifs allowed the essence of landscape to reveal itself. Keith wrote extensively on the transcendental if not mystical aspects of nature, and his works attracted a rapt following.[85] He owed a considerable intellectual debt to the esthetics of landscape expressed by the Rev. Thomas Starr King, who shared Keith's opinion that nature had

a religious aspect. Watkins's influence can also be seen in the work of a more prosaic artist, Thomas Hill (Fig. 87).

The great surveys employed a number of draughtsmen as well as photographers. Often the artists were illustrators of botanical and zoological specimens. Others were legitimate, well-known painters. In 1868/1869 Clarence King had on his survey the painter John Henry Hill, who was not on the official payroll. Typically the photographer, not the painter, was a volunteer, and King's hiring O'Sullivan suggests his admiration for photographs over other visual arts. Hill's work for the King Survey demonstrates how different were the results of

the artist's and the photographer's separate interpretations of the same motifs (Figs. 88, 89). The geologist's sketches of broad panoramas (Fig. 90), showing the demarcation of mountain ranges and the structure of the terrain are appealing to the modern eye for their spirited handling. Photographers, artists, and draughtsmen each created pictures to serve a different purpose, and each style makes its own appeal to twentieth-century tastes. Time has leveled each medium to the same esthetic plane.

F. V. Hayden had great admiration for the works of landscape artists and invited Sanford R. Gifford (Fig. 91) to accompany the expedition in 1870 and Thomas Moran in 1871/1872. The artists had much to offer W. H. Jackson, the staff photographer, who was relatively inexperienced with pure landscape. The daily routines of the artists and photographers were compatible, and Jackson spent much of his time absorbing principles of composition and design. Moran's drawings (Fig. 92) were gestural and painterly—rough pencil scribbles over which washes of color might be laid. They were evocative pictures rather than literal representations of the land. The artist and photographer began from opposite principles, a quality that no doubt enhanced their collaboration.

Contemporary reviews of Watkins's and Muybridge's work reveal how little photography critics knew of art theory. This did not prevent them, however, from judging photography by the esthetics of painting—principally the esthetic of picturesque romanticism. The Rev. C. B. Morton, writing on Watkins's mammoth-plate views, dwelled at length on the absence of human figures, which he felt might have been added to give an indication of scale and imply the role of human beings in the wilderness—Yosemite Valley. The suggestion that figures are required is reminiscent of the infant years of American landscape painting and its critics. Morton misunderstood Watkins's intent, which was to show Yosemite before the arrival of man by adopting a formal, classic composition. Another critic, E. L. Wilson, said of Wat-

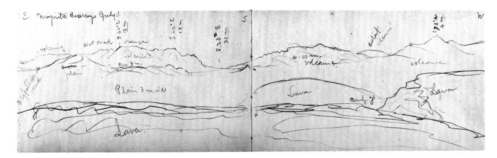

90. S. F. Emmons. Volcanic Landmarks, East Humboldt Mtns. Pencil drawing. **About** 1868. NA

91. Thomas Moran (1837–1926). Yellowstone River, below the Falls. Watercolor. 1871. 6⅛ x 4¼ in. CHMD

92. W. H. Jackson. Sanford R. Gifford on the Hayden Survey. 1870. H. ANS

kins's photographs, "In this instance, at least the camera is mightier than the pen." He later added: "The pen is weak, the camera is great."[86] Wilson meant not only to express his awe at the accomplishments of the photographs themselves but also to lament the absence of a critical framework in which to discuss them.

A decade after Watkins's first mammoth plates appeared, Muybridge's photographs were received with acclaim by his contemporaries. By that time American consciousness of landscape photography had been raised by the distribution of published editions. Muybridge's photographs were immedi-

ately accepted as the popular ideal of a successful picture; they even conformed to the widely accepted notion that photographs should resemble paintings. The newspaper *Alta California* observed that "we have just seen cloud effects as we see in nature or in oil painting, but almost never in a photograph."[87] E. L. Wilson, less ambiguous than in his critique of Watkins, compared Muybridge to the important British photographer G. W. Wilson, whose cloud and night effects were the quintessence of the picturesque in photography. So pervasive was the influence of the romantic style that Muybridge was felt to have "outdone all his com-

petitors,"[88] meaning Watkins, Muybridge's only true rival. Muybridge's flamboyant effects made Watkins's frontal class-cism seem old-fashioned and demanded a new set of critical values.

The eighties spawned a second generation of landscape photographers, whose work was cast in the mold of Muybridge's romanticism. W. H. Jackson was foremost among the new breed in the West, but also important were Fiske in Yosemite, F. J. Haynes in Yellowstone, and George Curtis at Niagara Falls. This generation catered to the tourist trade; gone was the meditative quality of the photographs from the era of exploration.

The Experimental Esthetic

One of the most important innovations of the first generation of outdoor photographers—journalistic and landscape photographers whose careers began about 1860—was to exchange the comfortable, predictable, and profitable life of the studio for the insecurity and unpredictability of the outdoors. At that early stage, when procedures and formulas had not been widely disseminated, the step was experimental, anticipating the direction photography would take in the future; by 1900 the majority of photographs were taken outdoors.

Partly as an adaptation to their new environment, the early landscape photographers actively experimented with technology and processes. The daguerreotype was limited in size and not easily replicated, but with the introduction of the wet-collodion plate, photographers were confronted for the first time with the practical possibility of making large-scale outdoor photographs. Since photographs could not be readily enlarged from the negative (although the "solar camera" made this possible in a crude way)[89] these mammoth plates were the only method of producing prints of great dimensions, by enlarging the image in the camera on the original negative.

Watkins pioneered in the use of the plate negatives, from which large prints for display in the parlor were made. In these mammoth-plate collodion negatives, eighteen by twenty-one inches, landscape was recorded on a scale and with a manifold detail not seen before. The most common parlor photographs were stereographs, which, when viewed through the stereoscope, appeared even larger than their size. Watkins visualized perfectly

the dynamic effect of a mammoth-plate landscape photograph displayed on the wall (Fig. 93) and the possibilities this idea presented for landscape photography. His example was followed by all the important landscape photographers of his time. C. L. Weed made mammoth views for Thomas Houseworth in 1864/1865; Eadweard Muybridge followed, using a similar camera in 1872; both worked in Yosemite. W. H. Jackson used a camera for twenty-by-twenty-four-inch plates in 1875, prob-

93. Unknown photographer. Detail of C. E. Watkins's display, Cleveland (?) Exposition. 1870. F. FL

94. John Semmendinger's patented (1873) mammoth-plate wet-collodion camera for field use, with Dallmeyer combination portrait-landscape lens

ably one of the type patented first in 1874 by John Semmendinger (Fig. 94).[90] After that it was a standard piece of equipment for any mountain photographer ambitious enough to carry and use it, of whom there were very few.

Making perfect negatives required immense perseverance and dexterity. The preparation of the wet-collodion negative had to be done on the spot. Polishing, coating, sensitizing, and developing—awkward with an eight-by-ten-inch sheet of glass—became positively ungainly when the plate reached mammoth size. Coating and sensitizing required that the photographer balance the plate in one hand while pouring the liquids over the glass surface with the other (Fig. 7). Watkins was particularly adventuresome in devising equipment and procedures for preparing negatives in remote areas.

The era of mammoth-plate photography was short. Because of the difficulty of handling the negatives, few photographers used the mammoth-plate equipment. In the eighties and nineties, when prepared dry plates came into common use, the inordinate cost of the mammoth plates further reduced interest in the process.

Like Watkins, O'Sullivan was aware of his inno-

vative role when he made the first photographs illuminated with magnesium light. The diaries of S. F. Emmons record the general excitement when the results of O'Sullivan's work in the Gould and Curry Mine were available in January 1868. William Bell, who took O'Sullivan's place on the Wheeler Survey of 1872, utilized his own dry-plate process, a method that revolutionized photography when it came into general use in the 1880s. As early as 1867 Muybridge was experimenting with his "sky shade," a device for reducing the overexposure of the sky, thus capturing clouds on the same negative as the landscape.[91] His photographs from the 1872 trip to Yosemite are graced with cloud-filled skies, much admired by public and critics but most certainly printed from a separate negative.

Experiments in photography also resulted in tangible esthetic changes. With his success in photographing the caves of the Gould and Curry Mine O'Sullivan added another image to the iconography of the medium. Similarly, Muybridge's clouds were thought by some critics to be the element that set his Yosemite photographs above those of Watkins. As a concession to his critics Watkins printed in clouds from separate negatives (Fig. 47, Pl. 19).

Perhaps the most revolutionary contribution of wet-plate landscape photography arose from a natural by-product of the photographic process: information about time. Many early photographers attempted to treat the passage of time very literally, attempting to stop motion (Fig. 95) like the makers of instantaneous views of London, Paris, and New York in about 1860. These photographs made a great impression on Muybridge, who later made his own studies of time and motion. In 1872 he was engaged by Leland Stanford to photograph Stanford's horse Occident galloping, in order to determine if all four legs were off the ground at once (Fig. 171). This Muybridge accomplished to his own satisfaction as well as Stanford's, opening a new field of photographing animals and humans in motion.

95. Lawrence and Houseworth, publishers. Montgomery St., San Francisco, from Market St., Instantaneous. About 1864. S. P

96. T. H. O'Sullivan. Green River, Colorado. Exposure A of six exposures. About 1872. F. LC

97. T. H. O'Sullivan. Green River, Colorado. Exposure B of six exposures. About 1872. F. LC

98. T. H. O'Sullivan. Green River, Colorado. Exposure C of six exposures. About 1872. F. LC

Landscape photographers also became involved with documenting the passage of time. O'Sullivan and Bell (Figs. 76–78), for example, made series of photographs over several months to illustrate King's theory of catastrophism and Emmons's theory of mechanical geology. These illustrate both geological and real time. On one occasion O'Sullivan took a remarkable set of six negatives from the rim of Flaming Gorge canyon on a single day (Figs. 96–98). They draw attention to the most elementary principle of photography: the role played by light as the essential force in the process. Textures, details, and entire forms metamorphose as the light changes. The precise reasons for O'Sullivan's making the series are unknown, but their implications for the potential of photography are great.

Watkins concerned himself with similar matters quite removed from conscious experiment but similarly related to the natural processes of photographing landscape. He photographed El Capitan (Figs. 44, 99, Pl. 2) over several years from nearly the same point of view. Although the time period is longer than O'Sullivan's—the earliest views was made in 1865 or 1866 and the latest in about 1880—the resulting series suggests many of the same effects prompted by O'Sullivan's sequence at Flam-

changes course slightly, some trees fall, others grow from adolescence to maturity; all are symbols as well as real evidence of the transience of the landscape.

The possibility of capturing motion and thereby isolating units of time was one of the most significant and influential accomplishments of nineteenth-century photography. However unlikely it might seem to find landscape photography relevant to stop-action photography, nature did change with time, and the earliest landscape photographers seemed fascinated to record the process. When the motion of a waterfall or stream could be stopped (Fig. 50) a new factor entered the esthetics of landscape photography.

99. C. E. Watkins. El Capitan. About 1880. I. P

ing Gorge. Watkins's photographs are about geological time governing the ecology of a mountain valley. Changes in the growth of trees and in the course of the stream bed are recorded here, as subtle as the changes in patterns of light and the modeling of shape in the O'Sullivan series. Watkins's views of El Capitan suggest how powerful were the forces in nature that caused visible change over a span of just a few years. The river

Landscape and the Published Photograph

100. T. H. O'Sullivan. Lake Marian. Title page and frontispiece in Clarence King, *Three Lakes: Marian, Lall, and Jan and How They Were Named*, 1870. NYPL

Before the availability of factory-prepared dry plates in the 1880s, the making of photographs required an immense amount of handwork. Polishing the glass plate, coating it with collodion, sensitizing the collodion with silver nitrate, and developing were all carried out in the field at the time of the exposure (Figs. 68–75), requiring manual dexterity on the part of the photographer (Fig. 7). Commercial processing laboratories did not exist, and the early outdoor wet-plate photographers were lucky to have even one assistant. Photographers of the 1860s and 1870s were aware of the pioneering aspect of their work, and they uniformly took great pride in it. Watkins, Muybridge, O'Sullivan, Jackson, and Russell manufactured their photographs with the care of master craftsmen. Their prints were meant to be appreciated as

esthetic creations, not just as ephemeral records of topography or geology, and almost immediately the photographs were recognized as works of value and beauty. Pride in workmanship was taken so seriously that Muybridge, through his agents, objected to the display of an imperfect portfolio of his prints in the show window of Thomas Houseworth's publishing firm. Angry words were exchanged over whether the prints were flawed in the publishing or through use.[92]

Photographs of the western landscape were enthusiastically received when they were shown around in New York, Washington, Boston, and New Haven by members of the King Survey in the winter of 1869. King carried from place to place a bulky portfolio of O'Sullivan photographs on heavy eighteen-by-twenty-four-inch mounts that weighed twenty to thirty pounds. It was not long before geologizing landscape photographs were being appreciated as photographs rather than as illustrations of nature. The best evidence is *Three Lakes*, a Christmas book of King's poetry illustrated with O'Sullivan's photographs (Fig. 100).[93]

King was not the only survey leader to have a sense of the worth of the photograph. F. V. Hayden instructed the director of the Academy of Natural Sciences in Philadelphia that the album of photographs by W. H. Jackson he was presenting to them should be kept in the library under special restrictions, explaining that "it is not a book to be handled by everyone."[94]

As early as 1863 Oliver Wendell Holmes, one of the most forceful early critics of photography, wrote of Watkins's photographs in language that could have been used to describe old master prints. He noted that they were "clear *yet soft*, vigorous in the foreground, delicately distinct in the distance,"[95] a description that could have fit an etching by Thomas Moran. Holmes was describing the criteria for a well-made albumen print: no deep, murky shadows to obscure details of texture and a wispy impression of the distant horizon, like a Chinese landscape painting.

The photographic printing paper was coated with egg albumen, which acted as a binder for the light-sensitive silver nitrate. The latent image on the paper was developed by the direct action of the sun, which caused the image to appear within fifteen to thirty minutes. The glass negative and the albumen paper together were put into the printing frame, which had a hinged door at the back that could be opened to check the progress. No chemicals were used in the developing process. The image turned first a deep purple, then reddish brown when the paper was immersed in a bath that neutralized the light-sensitive salts. The print was then washed with water and toned in gold to restore richness. Insufficient toning resulted in an anemic sepia print, while overtoning caused a print with dense shadows lacking texture and detail and an absence of the "clear, yet soft" quality prized by Holmes and other connoisseurs of photography.

An eighteen-by-twenty-one-inch print like those made by Watkins, Muybridge, and Jackson from their mammoth plates might require an hour to print, fix, tone, and wash. No mechanization was possible at any step of the process, and no chemical shortcuts had been invented. Since there were no artificial sources of heat that would not damage the print, drying had to take place by air. Watkins's diary for 1864 suggests that a day's work might result in only fifteen finished prints; Jackson's diary records that it took him fifteen hours to produce as many. A lithographer working the same fifteen hours might be able to produce a thousand lithographs printed from stone, but when photographs were transferred to a stone for printing they were robbed of their resolution (Figs. 102, 103). The criteria for quality in a photograph were similar to those for any fine print medium in which image quality is partly the result of craftsmanship.

High standards were upheld by photographers employed by the government surveys—contrary to what might be expected, since they were hired for scientific documentation. On the King Survey O'Sullivan made the first rough proofs in the field.

Several times a year he shipped the glass plates back to Washington, where they were received by the photographer to the Treasury Department, L. E. Walker, who appears to have had the only government studio in full-time service. Walker or an assistant would scratch a number in the negative and make proof prints for immediate distribution. When O'Sullivan was East in the winter of 1869, he made a few photographs which were distributed to influential members of Congress, like Senator John Conness, who was instrumental in securing support and funds for the survey.[96] A similar procedure was followed when O'Sullivan worked for the Wheeler Survey, although for Wheeler O'Sullivan produced enough prints to be bound uniformly into volumes, a more useful format than the loose prints from the King Survey. In 1875 when Wheeler commissioned bound volumes of photographs to accompany a limited number of published reports of his activity, O'Sullivan produced 2500 prints required for the fifty sets with fifty photographs each.[97] O'Sullivan also printed sets of fifty stereographs each year between 1871 and 1874. These were produced in small numbers, and no complete set from any year survives in the public archives.[98] In 1875 a boxed set of fifty stereographs selected from the 1871–1874 seasons were produced by O'Sullivan in an edition of fifty. Later these negatives were given to the firm of E. and H. T. Anthony in New York, who supplied prints to the general public. By this time, however, interest had fallen off, and Anthony complained of selling few copies.[99]

The most significant achievement of collodion negatives printed on albumen paper was their adaptation to the illustration of books. In the 1840s and 1850s the technology of making prints from negatives was not sufficiently advanced to encourage more than a few dozen isolated attempts to illustrate books with original photographs.[100] Those pioneering attempts were admirable, but the actual photographs were not good illustrations in spite of their great beauty (Fig. 14) because of

their lack of uniformity and resolution. In the 1860s methods for making uniform, permanent albumen prints progressed to maturity, and books illustrated with photographs proliferated yet remained less common than other types of illustrated books.

The rise of landscape photography occurred at the same time as the increased use of original photographs to illustrate books. The history of landscape photography was itself chronicled in published pictures. Josiah D. Whitney's *The Yosemite Book* (1868), of which two hundred fifty copies were illustrated with fifty original photographs by Watkins and four by W. Harris, comprised the report of Whitney's survey of Yosemite. It was among the first American books devoted entirely to photographs of landscape, work that duplicated in smaller format Watkins's informally published portfolios, which appeared as early as 1863. For his portfolios Watkins had used a photograph of a drawing by Fulgencio Seraqui, San Francisco's professor of penmanship and drawing, to simulate a title page (Fig. 101). Watkins did not publish his mammoth-plate photographs in an edi-

101.
Fulgencio Seraqui. Title page in C. E. Watkins's album of photographs presented to Ernest Frignet. Ink on paper. About 1863. HEH

102.
Photolithograph after T. H. O'Sullivan. Detail of Tufa Bank—Anaho Island—Pyramid Lake, Nevada. Published in King Survey report. 1875. NYPL

103.
T. H. O'Sullivan. Detail of Tufa Rocks, Pyramid Lake, Nevada. 1868. NA

tion but rather included the title page as an amenity in the sets he sold before his bankruptcy in 1873/1874.

King never published the photographs from the Fortieth Parallel Survey in an edition as Wheeler did for the One Hundredth Meridian Survey; the King Survey photographs therefore do not exist in uniform sets. While King had the photographs put on mounts with the survey imprint, uniform captions were never included, and it is difficult to identify many of the subjects. Stereographic cards produced for the King Survey in 1872 received such limited circulation that groups of more than a handful are rare.

For reasons unknown, King decided to use lithographs drawn after O'Sullivan's photographs to illustrate the final reports of his survey (Figs. 102, 103). While the drawings were made with fidelity to the originals, they lack the nuances of the original photographs. Wheeler utilized lithographs in his second and subsequent survey reports, and the record photographs appeared in a separate atlas volume.

Muybridge became involved in publishing very soon after Watkins. The results of his 1867 expedition to Yosemite were used to illustrate the first guide book to Yosemite by John S. Hittel, *Yosemite: Its Wonders and Its Beauties* (1868). It contains twenty original photographs reduced from Muybridge's series of half-plate negatives. The revenue from that enterprise must have contributed to launching Muybridge on his career in landscape photography, as well as to giving him a showplace to reveal how different stylistically his work was from Watkins's and Weed's.

In 1871 the Boston photographer John Soule published Professor Samuel Kneeland's *The Wonders of Yosemite Valley and of California*. The ten original photographs mounted into its pages are curious because there is no evidence that Soule, a talented landscape photographer (Figs. 28, 29), was ever in California, since no general body of California work was issued under his imprint. Yosemite is the only site in California to appear in photographs published by Soule. Landscape photographers generally photographed along the routes to their destinations, and the absence of such photographs in Soule's published work suggests that he might have purchased the negatives from a California photographer, not an uncommon transaction. The photographs have a strong stylistic affinity to Muybridge's work, some of which was still in the hands of Thomas Houseworth, who, typically, did not give credit to the actual author.

A. J. Russell's *The Great West Illustrated* (1869), published by the Union Pacific Railroad, was perhaps the most ambitious nongovernment publishing venture to be illustrated with photographs (Pls. 89-100). Its rarity today suggests that it either was not offered for general sale or that it was extraordinarily expensive. The fifty imperial-size photographs are each briefly described, making it a practical guide to the landscape between Omaha and Salt Lake City.

F. V. Hayden wrote a text to accompany photographs by Russell published under the title *Sun Pictures in the Rocky Mountains* (1870). It contained unsatisfactory reduced versions of Russell's *Great West Illustrated* plates and was one of the most common books of western landscape photographs. Its popularity contributed immensely to the public awareness of photography as a medium for landscape art.

Among the publications with the most significant lasting influence was W. H. Jackson's *Yellowstone's Scenic Wonders* assembled for Hayden in 1871 and *Photographs of the Yellowstone National Park and Views in Montana and Wyoming Territories* of 1873. Neither is truly a published book; both were albums of photographs made in editions of unknown size—perhaps twenty-five to fifty sets—with printed title pages and the imprint of Hayden's *Geological and Geographic Survey of the Territories. Yellowstone's Scenic Wonders* was distributed to influential persons in Washington as a public-relations activity when Hayden was seeking to renew the appropriation for his survey. It was the first official publication of the great surveys to be bound in permanent form and to contain a letterpress title page and photographs. The photographs by O'Sullivan that King circulated around Washington and other eastern cities in 1869 were loose prints put on uniform mounts with the Fortieth Parallel Survey imprint, but they were not done up in the presentation volumes Hayden provided.

One of the last photographically illustrated books from the flowering of California landscape photography was *Sun Pictures in Yosemite*, published in Chicago in 1874. It is significant for the light it sheds on California photography a decade earlier. The majority of the plates are reduced copies of mammoth-plate views by C. L. Weed from 1864/1865; the authorship can be deduced by comparison with Weed's signed photographs.[101] Some of the photographs bear a strong resemblance to Muybridge's, but none are exact duplicates of Muybridge's mammoth plates. The tantalizing implication is that Weed and Muybridge were closely enough associated at one time to be included together in an anthology of Yosemite photographs. Conspicuously absent is work by Watkins or any of the many photographers who had visited Yosemite by the date of publication. The unifying element in the anthology was very likely Thomas Houseworth's firm, which had published Weed's negatives in the mid-sixties and with whom Muybridge had been associated.

Hayden's first album of Jackson photographs not only succeeded in gaining renewed funds for him but was also apparently a factor in Congress's declaring Yellowstone a national park. The success of the first set inspired a second, which was a persuasive visual record of the vast terrain Hayden had covered in the territories. Moreover, the two photograph albums helped to dispel the wilderness myths about Yellowstone and the Geyser Basins which had developed from popular public lectures like those of N.P. Langford.[102]

Attempts to publish the mammoth-plate photographs of Watkins, Weed, and Muybridge in portfolios were not as successful as the illustrated-book ventures. By 1866 Watkins had arranged all of his mammoth-plate negatives in a numbered sequence from one to approximately one hundred fourteen. The sequence comprised a walking tour of Yosemite, beginning with an entrance to the valley from the Mariposa Trail, a progress along the valley floor to the rock monuments and to the various falls in order of importance, and finally an ascent to remote sites on the rim, Sentinel Dome (Pl. 14 and Glacier Point (Pl. 17). Watkins made up sets as customers required them. Not a single complete set of all the images exists, and even individual prints are rare. Similarly, Muybridge in 1873 was represented by Bradley and Rulofson in offering fifty-one photographs of Yosemite, the Mariposa grove of giant trees, and the High Sierra surrounding Yosemite. The photographs were put on mounts with printed captions and numbers, which made them a much more reasoned publishing venture than Watkins's views. Nevertheless, not a single complete set of Muybridge's mammoth-plate views exists in one place, and as with the Watkins views, even small collections are rare.

Thomas Houseworth offered mammoth-plate photographs for sale in his 1869 catalogue. These were probably produced by the only three competent mammoth-plate photographers in San Francisco: Watkins, Weed, and Muybridge; yet identifying their individual contributions is difficult (Fig. 50). Houseworth must not have sold many of the Watkins and Muybridge plates, however; mammoth prints of their work under the Houseworth imprint are rarely found in public collections.

The rise of landscape photography in America coincided with the beginnings of a trade in fine published photographs, which were made with all the care traditionally given to making prints in other media. By 1875 viewing landscape photographs had become a national pastime, and the heroic publishing ventures of the sixties and seventies were weakened by the proliferation of work by less-talented photographers. The stereograph rose to phenomenal popularity, providing a market for the work of countless photographers.

The End of the Era

104. W. Henry Brown. Starvation Rock (New Mexico).
      About 1875. s. MMA

105. W. Henry Brown. Burro Alley, Santa Fe. About
      1875. s. MMA

The popularity of landscape photographs brought many competitors to the scene once dominated by Watkins, Muybridge, O'Sullivan, Russell, and Jackson, although some of the regions O'Sullivan photographed have remained unpopulated to this day. Photographers who did settle in the Southwest, among them W. Henry Brown in Santa Fe (Figs. 104, 105) and H. Buehman in Tucson (Fig. 106), were attracted to ethnology and local architecture. They rarely ventured into the canyons and high country because people were not interested in buying photographs of deserts and rocks, as the failure of O'Sullivan's publishing venture with Anthony demonstrated. Jack Hillers, who spent considerable time in New Mexico after 1873, made the greater part of his reputation as a photographer of Indians.[103] W. H. Jackson, too, spent progressively more time photographing Indians and sites of ethnographic interest, and it was not until Jackson visited the Grand Canyon in 1892 that a substantial series of landscape photographs of that region was again made. Photographers in Oregon, Washington, and Wyoming were largely involved with recording daily life rather than landscape, probably because those states drew few tourists, the primary customers for landscape views.[104]

California and Colorado were another matter. Several serious competitors to Watkins emerged after Muybridge left the field for his motion experiments. Among the competition were Andrew Price at Geyser Springs and J. J. Reilly in Marysville (Fig. 107), who made beautiful Yosemite views based more on the romantic style of Muybridge than the austere classicism of Watkins. S. C. Walker and G. Fagersteen, partners working out of Stockton, also sold a line of Yosemite views. Southern

106. H. Buehman. Panorama of Tucson, Arizona. About 1875. s. MMA

107. J. J. Reilly. Agassiz Column. About 1875. s. MMA

108. W. G. Chamberlain. Monument Creek, Garden of the Gods (Colorado). No. 110. About 1869. s. MMA

California was not fertile land for the camera, and men like A. C. Varela in Los Angeles and the partnership of Hayward and Muzzall, like their counterparts in Arizona and New Mexico, photographed subjects of local interest and avoided the quest of picturesque landscape motifs.[105]

Colorado, on the other hand, with its mountains and rock formations and easy access by railroad, supported the most landscape photographers in the late seventies and eighties. W. G. Chamberlain began making landscape views as early as 1869, the year Jackson made his excursion along the route of the newly opened Union Pacific Railroad. Chamberlain photographed the Garden of the Gods prior to Jackson's first season there with Hayden in 1873.[106] Chamberlain's work (Figs. 108, 109) is the equal of that of the California trio of Watkins, Muybridge, and Weed, who by 1866 had perfected their handling of mountain scenery. In the hands of lesser talents, however, the natural wonders became clichés. Colorado photographers J. Collier, Charles Weitfle, B. H. Gurnsey, J. Thurlow, and T. Hines made professionally competent photographs without the visual and philosophical references of the best California work[107] It was the beginning of the postcard esthetic in which the grandeur of nature was expected to compensate for the lesser photographers' lack of imagination.[108]

109. W. G. Chamberlain. Garden of the Gods (Colorado). No. 109. About 1869. s. MMA

Chronology

Russell photographs for Union Pacific Railroad

A. A. Hart photographs for Central Pacific Railroad

1868   Andrew Johnson impeached

1868–1877   Ulysses S. Grant President

1868   Muybridge enters photographs of Yosemite and Alaska, presumably made during 1867, for copyright; marks negatives "Helios"

Watkins awarded medal for landscape at Paris International Exposition; photographs in Oregon with painter William Keith

1869   Golden Spike driven at Promontory, Utah, completing the transcontinental railroad, 10 May

Jackson photographs along the railroad west of Omaha, his first extensive landscape work

Russell associated with King Survey for short time

1870   Watkins on Mts. Lassen and Shasta with Clarence King's Fortieth Parallel Survey; exhibits photographs in Cleveland

1870–1878   Jackson with F. V. Hayden Survey

1870   Louis Agassiz lectures in San Francisco

O'Sullivan with Lt. Comdr. Selfridge's Darien Expedition in Panama

Outdoor photographers begin to flourish in California (Andrew Price, J. J. Reilly, A. C. Varela, Hayward & Muzzall, and others)

1871, 1873, 1874   O'Sullivan with Lt. George Wheeler's One Hundredth Meridian Survey in Arizona, New Mexico, Utah, and Idaho

1871   E. O. Beaman replaces Jack Hillers on the Powell Survey midway down the Colorado River

T. J. Hines photographs on Barlow Survey in Montana (works lost?)

1872   Wm. Bell replaces O'Sullivan on the Wheeler Survey for one season

O'Sullivan photographs with King Survey in Montana (works lost?)

Clarence King in Yosemite with Albert Bierstadt

Muybridge makes series of 51 mammoth-plate negatives in Yosemite and the surrounding Sierra Nevada

President Grant signs bill making Yellowstone a national park, an act influenced by Jackson's Hayden Survey photographs

Jack Hillers photographs on Powell Survey along the Colorado River

Muybridge begins to photograph horses in motion for Leland Stanford

1873   Watkins, O'Sullivan, and Muybridge exhibit photographs at Vienna International Exposition

1873/1874   Financial panic; Watkins's bankruptcy; I. Taber begins printing from Watkins's "old series" negatives

1874   O'Sullivan photographs in the Canyon de Chelly, September

Muybridge kills his wife's lover

1875   Muybridge photographs in Central America

Jackson makes his first mammoth-plate negatives (20 by 25 inches)

O'Sullivan lives in Baltimore; makes prints for Wheeler Survey albums

1876   Jackson manages the Hayden display at the Centennial Exposition in Philadelphia; becomes avidly interested in Indians

F. J. Haynes begins career as official photographer of Yellowstone National Park

Commerce in landscape photographs flourishes in Colorado (Chamberlain, Thurlow, Collier, and others)

1877–1881   Rutherford B. Hayes President

1877   Ethnology begins to rival pure landscape as main interest of government outdoor photographers

1878   Jackson in Yellowstone, where he photographs using only dry plates

Muybridge photographs thirteen-part panorama of San Francisco; *The Horse in Motion* published

1879   The great surveys consolidated under one agency, the United States Geological Survey, under the leadership of Clarence King

Jackson Photographic Co., specializing in landscape and railroad photographs, established in Denver

1880–1885   The first golden age of American landscape photography begins to decline

1880   Watkins makes first trip to southern California

Muybridge in Europe; J. D. B. Stillman reissues *The Horse in Motion* in London without credit to Muybridge

1882   O'Sullivan dies of tuberculosis

1890   Watkins's eyesight failing

1891   Russell's eyesight failing

About 1896 Muybridge returns to his native Kingston-on-Thames, England

1902   Russell dies in Brooklyn

1904   Muybridge dies (he has been constructing scale model of the Great Lakes in his backyard, Kingston-on-Thames)

1906   San Francisco earthquake and fire; Watkins's collection of negatives and prints lost; the same fate presumably befalls other collections of prints and negatives

1916   Watkins dies in an asylum

1942   Jackson dies after a fall

Carleton E. Watkins

1829-1916

During the summer or fall of 1861 Watkins visited the Yosemite Valley with equipment for making mammoth-plate and stereoscopic photographs. Approximately seventy-five of the stereos on glass are extant, and about twenty-five mammoth plates have been identified.[109] Watkins took great pride in the work, captioning the stereos by hand on the mounts and carefully printing the mammoth negatives on albumen paper, which he then mounted on large cards and framed behind glass. These were displayed at his Yosemite Art Gallery in San Francisco in 1867 before being exhibited in the East (Fig. 93) and Europe (Fig. 110). The photographs are significant in the history of American landscape photography as the first body of work to systematically present the landscape as a wilderness before the arrival of man. They are not the first landscape photographs, but they are the first to present nature from a deliberately assumed artistic posture.

Charles Turrill, who knew Watkins in the last years of his life, reported that his friend had learned photography about 1854 in the studio of Robert Vance, San Francisco's most eminent daguerreian.[110] Both Watkins and C. L. Weed were working for Vance in the late fifties, when the wet-collodion process made the daguerreotype completely obsolete. Probably as a matter of financial survival the Vance studio became one of the first on the West Coast to adopt the new technique. The studio production—portraits, views of mines, and cityscapes—was not credited to the individual photographers, and it is difficult to establish the authorship of the early paper prints; none firmly ascribed to Watkins have been recorded. Weed, however, distinguished himself by 1859,[111] when he

110. Unknown photographer. Watkins's display, Paris International Exposition. 1868. F. SW

111. C. L. Weed. Vernal Fall. No. 15. Published by E. Anthony. 1859. s. MMA

reian photographer in the West with an interest in pure landscape.[114] Jones's 1500 views of the best-known sites between St. Joseph, Missouri, and Salt Lake City are among the very few series of serious daguerreotype landscapes. Jones's headquarters were in San Francisco in the mid-1860s, and he employed up to five operators to photograph for him. While the daguerreotypes themselves are lost, descriptions of them attest to Jones's real concern for the land. In order to photograph Yosemite in 1861 with such sensitivity to the form and structure of nature, Watkins must certainly have had experience with outdoor work, and Jones's studio was practically the only one in America with such a declared predilection.

Yet it is impossible to dismiss Vance's role in Watkins's training. Watkins's visual education might not have come from Vance, but it could have come through him. Vance advertised in 1859 that

113. E. J. Muybridge ("Helios"). Pi-wy-ack (Cataract of Diamonds). Vernal Fall. 350 Feet. Published by Cosmopolitan Gallery of Photographic Art. 1867. s. MMA

made an excursion along the American River and to Yosemite, making photographs that strongly influenced Watkins, who set his camera up at many of the identical sites in 1861. Weed was doubtless the author of the Yosemite views published by Edward Anthony in 1860.[112]

Watkins surfaced in 1861, as advanced technically and esthetically as any eastern photographer, but how and from whom he had learned landscape art is not clear. It is conceivable that he was apprenticed to a master landscape pioneer in San Francisco, but two of the city's most visible figures, G. R. Fardon and Vance, did not work in landscape.[113] Both did city views, mine scenes, and portraits of miners as well as daguerreotypes of the Pacific Coast Indians, subjects that do not figure in Watkins's work of the sixties.

J. Wesley Jones (Fig. 38) was the only daguer-

112. C. E. Watkins. Piwyac, or the Vernal Fall, 300 feet. Published by I. Taber. 1861. s. MMA

he stocked the largest inventory of stereoscopic photographs in San Francisco—over 600 views, including scenes from Egypt and the Holy land, the Orient, and "portions of the Eastern United States."[115] Indeed, the best landscape photographs —by Frederick Langenheim (Figs. 11, 23), Charles Soulier (Fig. 20), and Francis Frith (Fig. 21)—were available in glass stereoscopic views, the ideal medium for transmitting an image with fidelity and brilliance. It is conceivable that the most capable European and American photographers were Watkins's teachers, through the best possible mode of instruction, the photographs themselves.

Langenheim's glass prints of waterfalls and other natural formations were, as subjects, the most important American precursors to Watkins's Yosemite photographs. Yet Langenheim's style differed in that he attempted to create miniature "paintings" in the manner of a Doughty (Fig. 8), Cole, or a Durand (Fig. 9). His photograph of Marshall's Falls, near the Delaware Water Gap (Fig. 23), with its layering of textured rock and the forceful design in the tree intersecting the falls, is typical of the picturesque romanticism of contemporary painting. Langenheim colored the photographs by hand, reinforcing their effect as miniature paintings.

Soulier's and Frith's photographs would have been particularly interesting to Watkins, because those photographers worked under hardship circumstances similar to the ones Watkins himself would face in transporting his equipment into Yosemite on muleback. Frith's views of Egypt and the Holy Land, which Vance offered for sale, were especially relevant, because Frith had pioneered in the wet-collodion process under expeditionary circumstances.[116] Frith's first journey along the Nile in 1857 presented the problems of traveling with a complete darkroom. For him transportation was convenient; a boat took Frith within shooting range of his subjects; the problem of high temperature, however, was not diminished. The ruins of ancient Egypt emerging from sand dunes bear a curious similarity to the monuments in stone—Cathedral Rock (Pl. 13), Half-Dome (Pl. 16), and the Three Brothers (Pl. 5)—which rise like architectural monuments from the walls of Yosemite Valley in Watkins's work.

Charles Soulier's glass stereos of the Alps and Auguste Bisson's treatment of similar subjects in paper were also available to Watkins. Both those photographers showed great visual imagination revealing nature's private spots of beauty, such as ice caves and eccentrically shaped rock formations (Fig. 20).

European photographers were all concerned with the structure and form of nature as well as its picturesque outward appearance, a feature especially attractive to Langenheim. Through the glass stereoscopic views of Langenheim, Frith, Soulier, and others Watkins could have experienced the remote landscape of many different regions, just as Alexander von Humboldt suggested in *Cosmos*. Furthermore, nature assumed a life-size scale via the stereoscope (Fig. 12), allowing the viewer an illusion of stepping into the landscape. By whatever means Watkins received his visual education, in 1861 his eye equaled those of the most sophisticated landscape photographers in the world. He appears to have digested the experience of the European landscape masters and added to it his own remarkably independent style based on the search for order and stability in nature.

Watkins made his 1861 trip to Yosemite as a gesture of flamboyant competitiveness with C. L. Weed (Figs. 40, 111), whose 1859 photographs he was determined to better. Ironically, Watkins, himself (Fig. 112) was competitively pursued in 1867 by Eadweard Muybridge (Figs. 45, 50, 113), who set his camera up on the same site at the Vernal Falls as Weed and Watkins had earlier in the decade.

In 1861 in Yosemite Watkins was mastering his equipment—some negatives are streaked, suggesting his skills were still latent—and seeking an esthetic stand. His mammoth-plate camera was unusual for its time and was not even commercially available. Watkins's was made to order in San Francisco, probably by a skilled cabinetmaker, since the body consisted of a wooden box fitted with an opening for the lens in the front and for the ground-glass plate in the back. No American field photographer before Watkins is reported to have worked with such equipment, nor was it marketed until after the Civil War. Watkins also used the relatively portable stereoscopic camera for studies of rocks (Fig. 114), trees, and rivulets (Fig. 115)—subjects more accessible with a small-format camera.

114. C. E. Watkins. El Capitan, 3,600 Ft. No. 118. Before 1866. s. MMA

115. C. E. Watkins. Cascade below the Vernal. No. 1079. Before 1867. s. MMA

116. Francis Frith. Beaulieu Priory. About 1856. s. p

Watkins's first Yosemite views are recognizable among the many photographs he made between 1862 and 1880. In 1861 he hesitated to prospect for the point of view to perfectly reveal his subject but rather coyly sighted through trees and over rivers and lakes in a manner typical of the picturesque romanticism Watkins would have seen in European stereoscopic views. The same approach was common among British photographers like Frith, whose Beaulieu Priory (Fig. 116) is a monument of crumbling stone not unlike the ones Watkins encountered in Yosemite. Watkins's 1861 photographs share with Frith's a methodical balancing of the primary subject with an unrelated element in nature (Pls. 2, 3)—in Frith's priory, the gnarled tree. Oliver Wendell Holmes, the author, wit, and coiner of the word *stereograph*, observed Watkins's affinity for the foreign views when he noted in 1863 that Watkins's stereos were "a perfection of art which compares with the finest European work."[117]

The stereoscopic camera (Fig. 13) conveyed a vivid sense of space, and in 1861 Watkins's eye was much more experienced in composing for the stereoscope than for the mammoth-plate camera (Fig. 94). Many of the mammoth views, such as Bridal Veil Falls (Fig. 117), were made simultaneously for the stereoscope (Fig. 118). The mammoth size transmits less of a sense of the sculptural form of the rocks, which are utterly three-dimensional in the small picture viewed through the stereoscope. During the 1861 season Watkins composed many of his mammoth views with the long side of the plate horizontal, as in the stereograph, which could only be made that way, since the stereo pairs had to be side by side. Watkins's concentration on the stereograph appears to have impeded his progress with the mammoth-plate camera, since the incredible sense of space inherent in the stereo did not require the search for special vantage points to best reveal sculptural forms. Watkins made almost all of his first mammoth views from sites more receptive to stereoscopic treatment, which meant they were not always the best viewpoints for the large plates.

Watkins's first series in Yosemite was flawed in minor ways compared to photographs he made later. Nevertheless, they struck wonder in even his most seasoned contemporaries. W. H. Brewer, Clarence King's good friend and later an associate of Timothy O'Sullivan on the King Survey of the fortieth parallel, noted with astonishment that "a photographer packed in his apparatus on mules and took a series of the finest photographs that I have ever seen."[118] Charles R. Savage, an important photographer of Salt Lake City, was astounded by Watkins's "carrying such huge baths, glasses, etc. on mule back."[119]

About 1866 Watkins's style became more cerebral as he abandoned the elementary picturesqueness of his 1861 work. The transition can be seen, in part, in a series of photographs of El Capitan made between 1861 and 1866.[120] In 1861 Watkins presented the rock horizontally (Pl. 2), which diminishes its sublime verticality; moreover, his point of view suggests a paper-thin silhouette and minimizes the sculptural form. The shell of the fallen tree at the left assumes more graphic importance, as though Watkins was attempting to impart equal stature to both the tree and the mountain. C. L. Weed was in Yosemite again in 1864/1865 and made a number of mammoth-plate views that directly competed with Watkins's 1861 series and initiated a remarkable cycle of action and reaction between the two photographers. Weed seems to have made the first vertical view of El Capitan in 1865 (Fig. 43), which inspired Watkins to make his own upright version (Fig. 44). This second El Capitan, made sometime between 1864 and 1866, conveys the subtlety of the rock surface and subordinates the picturesque elements in the surrounding landscape to the main subject—the canyon wall. The site was well chosen, and Watkins would return to it repeatedly, photographing the rock face in many different lights (Fig. 99). He also confronted other features of the valley head-on, choosing the most revealing approaches to the Three Brothers (Pl. 5), Cathedral Spires, and the Sentinel. In these he again subdued the overtly picturesque elements and avoided the deliberate romanticism he expressed in 1861. The Mirror View of El Capitan (Pl. 6) has romantic overtones in the mirror motif yet still retains a formal sense of design that focuses on the rock face itself rather than dispersing the center of interest through competing elements subordinate to the main subject.

The only access to the high regions around the rim of Yosemite Valley was through wilderness, since the trails off the main routes from Mariposa and Couterville had not been developed. Before 1866 Watkins confined himself to making photographs from the valley floor and along the Mariposa Trail; most of these are dominated by obvious motifs—waterfalls, rock formations, and river views. By 1864 more complex and subtler subjects such as Up the Valley (Pl. 8), which describes the shape of the sky in the dramatic void between the rocks as well as the rocks themselves. The field of grass assumes the same compositional weight as

the trees. The photograph was composed to balance left against right, horizontal tension against vertical, and to delineate space by carefully defined planes that recede from the center to infinity. It is a work in which classical order and romantic eccentricity confront one another, and in Watkins's attempt to unify the conflicting elements, rocks, trees, fields, and grass are juxtaposed to disclose the infinite order of nature rather than its paradoxes.

Watkins went to the high regions around Yosemite Valley in 1866, again in the footsteps of Weed (Fig. 43) but before Muybridge made his "Helios" views from the valley floor in 1868. He traveled with Clarence King, James T. Gardner, and others of the Whitney Survey party. Changes in Watkins's style might be ascribed in part to this experience.[121] Watkins's views of Yosemite Valley from Sentinel Dome (Pl. 18) and the pendants Lyell Group (Pl. 20), and Merced Group (Pl. 21), both taken from the Sentinel Dome, subordinate their main subjects in the distance in very unconventional ways but present elegantly curved rock formations in the foreground. The pendants represent a bold reconsideration of the principles of picturesque romanticism. Yosemite Falls is the central element in the Valley seen from Sentinel Dome, yet because of its diminutive size and great distance from the viewer, it does not seem to dominate the composition. The photograph is methodically structured into five overlapping planes—sky, horizon, valley walls, trees, and foreground—each of which is important to the total effect of communicating the infinite gradations from pebble to mountain. Moreover, Watkins developed a style of printing his negatives in which the most distant parts are faint. His atmospheric perspective is not unlike that achieved by the seventeenth-century French etcher Jacques Callot, who invented that method for his

118. C. E. Watkins. Po-ho-no, Bridal Veil. 1861. S. IMP/GEH

copperplate etching, and also bears a similarity to Chinese landscape painting.

By 1867 Watkins had a reputation with the cognoscenti of both coasts. He was probably the most experienced landscape photographer in California, where outdoor work flourished unhindered by the Civil War. In 1864 he had been honored by the friends of Ernest Frignet, and a selection of the Yosemite views were included in a lavish album presented to Frignet when he returned to France to write his history of California. During the summer of 1863 Watkins was perhaps in Yosemite when Albert Bierstadt made his visit there. Bierstadt used the Grizzly Giant (Fig. 86, Pl. 24) as an apparent model for his painting of the same subject (Fig. 85). Watkins's photographs had also strongly impressed Thomas Starr King, Bierstadt's traveling companion, and Fitz Hugh Ludlow, two men very influential in popularizing nature in literature.[122] In 1866 Watkins had worked with Josiah Whitney, Clarence King, and W. H. Brewer in Yosemite and had enclosed a reproduction of their map—the first one drawn of Yosemite—in his albums and portfolios. He had been acknowledged a master by Oliver Wendell Holmes, the foremost critic of photography of the mid-nineteenth century and, moreover, had been the subject of two extensive commentaries in *The Philadelphia Photographer*, the leading journal of photography in America.[123] Despite all the acclaim, however, Watkins had not copyrighted his photographs, an unfortunate oversight, in view of Thomas Houseworth's triumph at the Paris Exposition of 1867.

The Paris incident was probably what prompted Watkins, Muybridge, and Hart, the three most talented photographers in northern California, to identify their work after 1867. Watkins began putting his eight-by-twelve-inch views on mounts bearing the copyright imprint along with a handwritten notation that Hardy Gillard was his sole agent. He also had his stereo mounts printed with the copyright insignia and his name. Watkins was in the enviable position of being the leading California

landscape photographer, and other men suddenly found it necessary to include landscape in their repertories; Eadweard Muybridge applied for copyright to his first views of Yosemite in 1868, and others entered the scene by 1870. Among the newcomers were J. J. Reilly, who published Yosemite views out of Marysville, and Andrew Price, who established himself at Geyser Spring in the Napa Valley.

By 1867 Watkins had established his Yosemite Art Gallery (Fig. 119) at 429 Montgomery Street in San Francisco. The name was doubtless chosen to capitalize as much as possible on the unexpected spotlight thrown on American landscape by foreigners, to define the work for which Watkins himself wanted to be known, and to distinguish his

119. C. E. Watkins's advertisement in the *San Francisco Directory*, 1873.

120. C. E. Watkins. Laying the Corner Stone of the New City Hall, February 22, 1872, s. MMA

work dramatically from those photographers who specialized in genre subjects, townscapes, and railroad views. Watkins's work, however, took an unexpected direction. While other photographers were making landscape photographs to compete with him, he, in turn, entered for copyright a series of cityscapes, including impressive instantaneous views (Fig. 120), for which Muybridge had gained his reputation.

Watkins had established himself by photographing nature as it might have appeared before the arrival of man, but he had also photographed regularly around San Francisco, recording scenes like the parade on 4 July 1864, which he entered for copyright in 1867 along with other city views and panoramas.

In 1868 he traveled up the Pacific Coast to Oregon with the landscape painter William Keith.[124]

He made a few photographs of the logging towns and county seats and continued to record the elemental forms of nature. After the Oregon trip he had enough negatives of industry, town, and landscapes to issue his own "Pacific Coast" series; that caption, printed on the photographs was doubtless meant to place them in competition with Houseworth's series "Scenery of the Pacific Coast." Watkins's mammoth-plate Oregon views of 1868 are the zenith of his landscape work. His career changed substantially after 1873/1874, and the Oregon series represents his highest achievement as a photographer of pure landscape. He was to later become involved in strictly commercial work, such as the 200 views he made in 1880 for a Los Angeles fruit grower.[125]

Oregon had been little photographed before Watkins's arrival, and he was met there by a subtle and elegant landscape that had rarely been the subject of pictures of any kind. For Watkins it was an experience like visiting Yosemite in 1861, when he had been one of the first picture makers to enter the territory. Compositionally, the Oregon photographs sustain the direction of the views of Yosemite from Sentinel Dome (Pls. 14, 18, 20, 21); in the Yosemite pictures Watkins did not use a simple formula but imposed his sense of order and design on nature. He accomplished the effect of unity by choosing points of view that presented the viewer with a visual harmony of overlapping shapes, planes, and masses of land.

Watkins was methodical about using the horizon as the structural foundation of his photographs. He rarely created dramatically shaped horizons but rather photographed gentle undulations that intersect key vertical elements at carefully chosen points (Pls. 28, 29). He did not eliminate curves or diagonals but simply subordinated them to the horizontal lines; the treatment caused the interplay between vertical and horizontal so characteristic of classical art in other media. By imposing his own strict sense of order on the landscape, Watkins tempered his basically romantic instincts;

his formalism was at odds with his eminently picturesque subjects.

In 1870 Clarence King asked Watkins to accompany his party, which included Samuel F. Emmons and the painter Gilbert Munger, on the ascent of Mts. Shasta and Lassen (Fig. 83). O'Sullivan, who had been King's photographer on the Fortieth Parallel Survey in 1868/1869, was with Comdr. Selfridge in Panama. But Watkins was confident that he could work with King; he had done so in 1866 in Yosemite, where he had made his most direct and successful photographs of rocks and trees.

King (Fig. 67) was a dilettante and a student of John Ruskin as well as a practicing geologist. Moreover, he had deep religious convictions grounded in transcendentalism and John Ruskin's philosophy of art. King looked to nature for affirmation of his religion, his art, and his profession, and he clearly set an unusual tone, for his geological expeditions were as much involved with the esthetics of mountaineering as with the science of geology.[126] S. F. Emmons wrote his brother, Arthur, his impressions upon reaching the summit of Shasta. The report was couched entirely in philosophical rather than scientific terms. King's biographers speak of his discoursing on art and literature around the evening campfire during the Fortieth Parallel Survey.[127]

Watkins's Lassen photographs (Pl. 23) express the particular concerns of King. Emmons described to his brother King's eager participation in the photography, noting in passing that Watkins brought along three times as much gear as O'Sullivan had employed on the Fortieth Parallel Survey.[128] King is said to have personally blazed the route for Watkins to get one particularly good (but unidentified) view which required the whole party's staying an extra night. The chiseled rock formations and intricately layered snow-covered mountains were quite challenging as subjects. Yosemite generously provided perfect viewpoints, while at Shasta and Lassen (Fig. 83) the best sites were more elusive.

Clarence King said that Watkins was the finest

photographer he knew, and Turrill said that he was "more of an artist than a businessman."[129] Both statements are true; despite acclaim on both coasts and his deep sensitivity, Watkin's business failed, presumably in the financial panic of 1873/1874. He lost all of his work up to that time to his creditors.[130] His negatives ultimately fell into the hands of I. W. Taber, who had operated a portrait studio in the same building as Watkins's studio (Fig. 121). Watkins had given numbers to all of his negatives up to that time, so the progress of his career is divided into the relatively well defined "old series," made between 1861 and 1873/1874, and a "new series" that spanned the rest of his life.

The "old series" consisted of approximately 114 mammoth-plate negatives of Yosemite, of which about sixty have been identified. He also made another 2000 stereographic photographs, of which only a fraction are known. Watkins probably

121. C. E. Watkins. Yosemite Art Gallery, Montgomery St., San Francisco. About 1875. s. LL

85

adopted the system of numbering the prints some-time after 1864 since extant sets of photographs from the 1861 trip to Yosemite are not numbered. It is conceivable that the early views satisfied Watkins less after he had accomplished the extraordinary work of 1866 and that the glass plates were reused for other negatives. So few copies of the 1861 views survive that only a scant number could have been sold when the negatives were first made.[131] Taber published some but not all of Watkins's earliest stereo views from Yosemite, but none of the earliest mammoth-plate views with Taber's imprint are recorded, which further suggests that Watkins could have eradicated the early negatives to reuse the glass. For whatever reason, the 1861 views neither fell into Taber's hands nor did Watkins himself print from them later. He did, however, make reduced copy negatives from old prints. During the 1870s and 1880s Taber printed from Watkins's sixty or seventy best negatives, all

122. C. E. Watkins. Victoria Regia—Golden Gate Park, San Francisco. About 1875. S. MMA

of which were lost in the earthquake and fire of 1906.[132]

Watkins's second decade as a landscape photographer was spent remaking his lost work. He returned to Yosemite and initiated the "new series," visiting the sites and subjects he had found to be the most popular of his first series and photographing from the very same sites. Many times the photographs are so similar that only the growth of plants and erosion of land betrays the elapsed time (Figs. 44, 99, Pl. 2). El Capitan changed through natural causes, but other subjects, such as Sugar Loaf, saw the intrusion of man-made structures—the Hotel La Casa Nevada, which was built between the Vernal and Nevada falls. At the very moment he was feeling intense competition from Muybridge, Watkins was forced into the artistic stagnation of repeating himself.

Between 1870 and 1875, the role of the outdoor photographer began to change as a result of marketing developments. Prior to 1869 outdoor photographs were made by relatively small numbers of men who photographed both what attracted them as artists and what they felt would be interesting to a hypothetical body of clients; an example is Watkin's Victoria Regia (Fig. 122). The clients were hypothetical because the commerce in photographs was at an infant stage, and photographers did not have firm guidelines for what they should photograph. In 1867 the raves of the European press responding to the "Houseworth" and Watkins exhibitions at the Paris International Exposition gave the impression that the world was eager for wilderness landscape views. The marketplace proved otherwise, however, and Watkins had to adjust to reality. The completion of the transcontinental railroad in 1869 brought a steady stream of travelers along a very specific route, creating a demand for what soon came to be a set of very standard subjects, such as Hanging Rock (Pl. 90) and Finger Rock along the route of the Central Pacific Railroad. This was a very limiting factor for a photographer because, as the markets for photographs

became more predictable, the number of profitable subjects became smaller. Consequently, a photographer who sought out subjects far from the routes tourists traveled ran the risk of selling fewer photographs. When motifs became so standardized that taste and judgment were no longer required of the photographer, second-rate talents were sent out with specific instructions about what to photograph. Outdoor photography became a lucrative business as increasing numbers of less discriminating tourists traveled the new rail routes throughout the West. Bland and uninspired landscape photographs came to dominate the supply, and landscape photography was burdened with the output of mediocre talents whose works offend any sensitive eye.

Watkins's future was seriously damaged by the pattern of demand. He was by temperament a risk-taker and, judging from his extant work, preferred to take photographs he perceived as beautiful rather than those which were good commercial prospects. He failed to understand that tourists bought views of what they had seen rather than sights far from the normal routes.

In 1873, just prior to his bankruptcy, Watkins traveled to Utah with William Keith to photograph along the route of the Central Pacific Railroad, which connected with the Union Pacific there. He produced a view of Salt Lake City (Fig. 71), composed with the intensity of his Yosemite views of 1866. He described a universe composed of a carefully graduated continuum from the banal and the specific in the foreground to the majestic and the general in the distance. The Salt Lake City photograph consists of carefully constructed planes, the foreground being a tightly visualized zig-zag of fences and fields which lead to the middle ground containing the city itself, which in turn gives way to a layer of haze and then to the planes of the mountain and the sky, a design comparable to his views of Yosemite Valley from Sentinel Dome (Pl. 14). Over one-third of the photograph consists of rail fences, a fieldstone wall, and a half-completed foundations. Watkins's photograph was carefully designed to convey the essence of the city in purely visual terms using many irrelevant facts of nature as the basic elements of his composition.

Also in Utah in 1873, Watkins made a photograph of Profile Rock in Echo Canyon (Pl. 27). A. J. Russell, W. H. Jackson, and C. R. Savage, among other photographers, had preceded Watkins to Echo, and most of the obviously picturesque rock formations there had already been photographed. Rather than photographing Hanging Rock, for which the visual possibilities were limited, Watkins recorded another formation that resembled the profile of a human face. The resulting composition communicated more than the anthropomorphic character of the rock. The railroad track gently leads the eye off into the distance and away from the compelling textures and shapes of the conglomerate rocks so that the photograph encompasses a vast but subtle range of effects. Profile Rock would probably never have been noticed by a traveler, which compromised the usefulness of Watkins's view to the Union Pacific Railroad; a tourist would have been more likely to remember a formation like Hanging Rock (Pl. 90).

Between 1875 and 1880 Watkins attempted a compromise between the diverging directions of the photographic illustrator and the artist deeply in love with nature. The influence of Bierstadt and King never disappeared, and Watkins continued to see compositions of great pictorial strength, always conceived with an intellectual vigor that removes them from the simplemindedly picturesque. His Storm on Lake Tahoe (Pl. 31) could be postcard romanticism in the hands of another artist, but Watkins's self-assured sense of visual order brought nature's drama into control.

The need to provide views of tourist attractions could not escape any landscape photographer. Watkins might have preferred to create in his photographs the illusion of virgin landscape before the arrival of civilization, but he did photograph such subjects as the logging works at Glenbrook Bay

123. C. E. Watkins. Central Pacific Railroad, Donner Lake. New series no. 1122. About 1880. M. P

and the trackage by which the Central Pacific Railroad descended from the Sierra Nevada in a series of switchbacks covered with snow sheds (Fig. 123). Watkins was a lifelong friend of railroad chief Collis P. Huntington, who made a flatcar available for him to transport his photographic van. While adequate as illustrations, the industrial views lack the brilliance of Watkins's pure landscape work.

In 1880 Watkins made his first trip to southern California,[133] where he produced a series that reveals the delicate balance he maintained between art and illustration. He methodically recorded the

Spanish missions at intervals along El Camino Real, but the flat deserts and bare hills did not inspire him as they had O'Sullivan in Nevada. His photograph of a Section of the Loop on the Southern Pacific Railroad (Fig. 124), perhaps made for the edification of Huntington, was accomplished with careful staging to present the special geometry he favored in pure landscape.

Throughout his career Watkins was interested in trees, as may be seen by their prominent role even in the 1861 Yosemite views (Pls. 1, 2). By 1866, if not before, he had begun to make tree portraits, the most famous of which is the Grizzly Giant (Fig. 86, Pl. 24). He studied several varieties of trees around Yosemite, most of them physically unspectacular. In southern California Watkins continued to savor interesting trees and as a result made a few pure landscapes on that trip (Pl. 33). As a group, and tree portraits (Pls. 24, 32, 33) are exceptional in the history of photography as early examples of the pursuit of pure form. Watkins always gave them their Latin names, such as *Yucca Dra-conis* (Pl. 33), which suggests that he also expected them to be visual documents for the use of scientists, as indeed they were for G. K. Gilbert, who wrote in his journal of taking a day in San Francisco to visit Watkins's gallery and listed the tree photographs he bought.[134]

While on his trip south, Watkins wrote to his wife, Frankie, "if this business don't give us a living we will go and squat on some government land and raise spuds."[135] Watkins had been married less than a year, an adventurous change for a man of

124. C. E. Watkins. Southern Pacific Railroad, Section of the Loop. New series no. 1135. About 1880. M. P

125. C. E. Watkins. Young Squid Catchers, Monterey. About 1880. H. MMA

126. C. E. Watkins. Children's Play Ground, Golden Gate Park, San Francisco. About 1885. H. MMA

ject. After the development of plates and lenses for recording motion without blur, seeking out unphotographed motifs replaced patience as the photographer's chief virtue. Watkins had both qualities, and he adapted to the change.

Ironically, just as Watkins was diverted from pure landscape, W. H. Jackson was about to establish his Denver studio, from which he would develop a worldwide reputation as a landscape photographer. In 1883 Jackson went to California and made views of Yosemite and the Del Monte Hotel, two of Watkins's favorite sites. Watkins was in the autumn of his career and could not radically change his work or his vision; Jackson was young and enterprising and eventually saw the commercial success Watkins found so elusive.

Watkins's landscape style of the mid-1880s focused on lesser subjects than the High Sierra and Yosemite. He worked often for landowners who commissioned photographs of their farms, ranches,

127. C. E. Watkins. The "Oakland" Leaving the Oakland Slip. About 1885. H. MMA

fifty-one. At about the time of his marriage he established an elaborate gallery on the New Montgomery Street side of the Palace Hotel. Frankie managed the shop, and Watkins employed one Chinese darkroom assistant. In the gallery he exhibited the mammoth-plate views of the "new series," which were often sold in black walnut frames (Fig. 93) and were the mainstay of the business.[136] Watkins changed his subjects as the times changed. When he photographed the Young Squid Catchers, Monterey (Fig. 125), Children's Play Ground in Golden Gate Park (Fig. 126), or the ferry "Oakland" Leaving the Oakland Slip (Fig. 127), the contemplative premises of his wilderness landscape were necessarily abandoned.

The greatest virtue of the early landscape photographer was patience enough to wait for the right light and absolute stillness on and around the sub-

and estates. Yet his views of mundane subjects could never look commonplace. The fields at the Berkshire Ranch (Fig. 128) near Sonoma have an almost meditative quality. He recorded not so much the simple two-dimensional designs of the plowed field as the complex visual interaction between fields for different crops. He played the plowed field against the orchard; sapling against full-grown tree; and furrow against levee. Such photographs show a person "in love with nature,"[137] the very words used by Watkins's biographer to describe the photographer's temperament.

Watkins apparently moved in the upper strata of California society, an unusual accomplishment for a photographer then. In 1878 he was discussing the merits of French claret wine with the geographer George Davidson; he was known to be invited in for gala balls at the ranches and estates he photographed; and he was given a retirement house by Huntington. By 1906 Watkins, blind, was led from his burning studio when the earthquake and fire struck San Francisco and destroyed his negatives and file of prints.[138] The negatives were then being printed with little success by Watkins's son, Collis, namesake of Huntington. The natural professional atrophy of his later years, compounded by the loss of his lifework, caused Watkins's career to remain in essential eclipse compared to the significance of his accomplishment and compared to the world-wide fame achieved by Muybridge and Jackson, both of whose careers might have been different had Watkins not broken ground for them.

128. C. E. Watkins. The Berkshire Ranch, Napa Valley. About 1885. I. P

PLATE 1. C. E. WATKINS. LAKE AH-WI-YAH, YOSEMITE. 1861. M. TVL

PLATE 2. C. E. WATKINS. TU-TOCH-ANULA, OR EL CAPITAN, 3,600 FT. HIGH, YOSEMITE. 1861. M. IMP/GEH

PLATE 3. C. E. WATKINS. DOWN THE VALLEY, YOSEMITE. NO. 37. 1861 (?). M. BPL

PLATE 4. C. E. WATKINS. CATHEDRAL SPIRES, YOSEMITE. 1861. M. IMP/GEH

PLATE 5. C. E. WATKINS. THREE BROTHERS, 4,480 FT., YOSEMITE. NO. 28. ABOUT 1861. M. AGS

PLATE 6. C. E. WATKINS. MIRROR VIEW, EL CAPITAN, YOSEMITE. NO. 38. ABOUT 1866. M. NYPL

677. El Capitan, 3,300 feet, Yosemite, Cal.

Photo, San Francisco.

PLATE 7. ATTRIBUTED TO C. E. WATKINS. PUBLISHED
BY I. TABER. EL CAPITAN, YOSEMITE. ABOUT
1870. M. MMA

PLATE 8. C. E. WATKINS. UP THE VALLEY FROM THE MARIPOSA TRAIL—EL CAPITAN AND THE CATHEDRAL GROUP, YOSEMITE. NO. 9. ABOUT 1866. M. NYPL

PLATE 9. C. E. WATKINS. MT. STARR KING, YOSEMITE. NO. 69. ABOUT 1866. M. AGS

PLATE 10. C. E. WATKINS. WASHINGTON COLUMN, 2,082
FT., YOSEMITE. NO. 81. ABOUT 1866. M. BPL

PLATE 11. C. E. WATKINS. RIVER VIEW TOWARDS NORTH DOME. YOSEMITE. ABOUT 1866. M. BPL

PLATE 12. C. E. WATKINS. VIEW ON THE MERCED, YOSEMITE. NO. 41. 1861. M. P

21. Cathedral Rock, 2,678 feet, Yosemite, Cal.

Photo, San Francisco.

PLATE 13. C. E. WATKINS. CATHEDRAL ROCK, 2,600 FT., YOSEMITE. NO. 21. PUBLISHED BY I. TABER. ABOUT 1866. M. MMA

PLATE 14. C. E. WATKINS. MERCED GROUP FROM THE SENTINEL DOME, YOSEMITE. NO. 97, 1866. M. P

PLATE 15A. C. E. WATKINS. ROCK STUDIES BETWEEN THE YOSEMITE FALLS. 1861. S. IMP/GEH

PLATE 15B. C. E. WATKINS. FROM THE FOOT OF THE UPPER FALL, YOSEMITE. ALBUMEN ON GLASS. 1861. S. IMP/GEH

PLATE 16. C. E. WATKINS. FIRST VIEW OF THE YOSEMITE VALLEY, FROM THE MARIPOSA TRAIL. ABOUT 1866. M. BPL

99. Yosemite Falls, from Glacier Point.   Photo, San Francisco.

PLATE 17. C. E. WATKINS. YOSEMITE FALLS, FROM
GLACIER POINT. NO. 99. PUBLISHED BY
I. TABER. ABOUT 1866. M. MMA

PLATE 18. C. E. WATKINS. YOSEMITE VALLEY FROM
SENTINEL DOME. NO. 93. ABOUT 1866. M. P

PLATE 19. C. E. WATKINS. YOSEMITE VALLEY FROM THE "BEST GENERAL VIEW." NO. 2. ABOUT 1866. M. AGS

PLATE 20. C. E. WATKINS. THE DOMES FROM SENTINEL DOME, YOSEMITE. NO. 94. 1866. M. SW

PLATE 21. C. E. WATKINS. THE DOMES FROM SENTINEL DOME, YOSEMITE. NO. 95. 1866. M. BPL

PLATE 22. C. E. WATKINS. THE HALF DOME FROM GLACIER POINT, YOSEMITE. NO. 101. ABOUT 1866. M. AGS

PLATE 23. C. E. WATKINS. LASSEN PEAK FROM THE SOUTH WEST (CALIFORNIA). 1870. F. IMP/GEH

PLATE 24.
C. E. WATKINS. GRIZZLY GIANT,
MARIPOSA GROVE, CALIFORNIA. NO. 110.
BEFORE APRIL 1864. M. BPL

PLATE 25.
C. E. WATKINS. MULTNOMAH
FALLS, COLUMBIA RIVER,
OREGON. 1868. M. UT

732   Agassiz Column, near Union Point.

PLATE 26. ATTRIBUTED TO C. E. WATKINS. PUBLISHED
BY I. TABER. AGASSIZ COLUMN, YOSEMITE.
ABOUT 1870. M. P.

705. Profile Rock, Echo Canon, Utah.   Photo, San Francisco

PLATE 27. ATTRIBUTED TO C. E. WATKINS. PUBLISHED BY I. TABER. PROFILE ROCK, ECHO CANON, UTAH. 1873. M. MMA

PLATE 28. C. E. WATKINS. CASTLE ROCK, COLUMBIA RIVER, OREGON. 1868. M. SU

PLATE 29. C. E. WATKINS. CAPE HORN, OREGON. 1868. M. SU

PLATE 30. C. E. WATKINS. WINTER VIEW OF CAPE HORN FROM BRIDAL VEIL, OREGON. ABOUT 1874. I. HB

PLATE 31. C. E. WATKINS. A STORM ON LAKE TAHOE (CALIFORNIA). 1880–1885. M. P.

PLATE 32. C. E. WATKINS. ARBUTUS MENZIESII PURSH. 1880–1885. M. MOMA

PLATE 33. C. E. WATKINS. YUCCA DRACONIS, MOJAVE DESERT (CALIFORNIA). ABOUT 1880. M. P

PLATE 34. C. E. WATKINS. MONTEREY, CALIFORNIA–PEBBLE BEACH. NO. 35. 1880–1885. M. P

Timothy H. O'Sullivan
About 1840-1882

129. Isaac Hayes. View of Glacier in Barden Bay, Whale Sound, North Iceland. 1861. s. P

O'Sullivan was born in New York to parents recently emigrated from Ireland. The family soon settled on Staten Island, and by his mid-teens O'Sullivan was commuting regularly to Mathew Brady's Fulton Street gallery. While nothing is known of his apprenticeship to Brady, he rose rapidly to a position of responsibility, first in the New York gallery and then in the Washington branch managed by Alexander Gardner.[139]

The twenty-one-year-old O'Sullivan was at Bull Run in 1861 as a cameraman in "Brady's Photographic Corps," where the battle "would have been photographed 'close up' but for the fact that a shell from one of the rebel fieldpieces took away the photographer's camera."[140] For the next fourteen years O'Sullivan continued to practice his precise art under the most consistently treacherous and demanding conditions yet confronted in the short history of photography.

Others had attempted wet-plate photography under hardship conditions. A string of government expeditions proved unsuccessful in their use of the medium, while other groups, such as the Lander Expedition to the western United States of 1858/1859 and the Hayes Expedition to Greenland in 1861 (Fig. 129) had only limited success. More important was the expeditionary photography carried out by the team of the painter William Bradford, who embarked via ship for the arctic regions at about the time O'Sullivan first went West. The

130. John Dunmore. View of the Semitsialik Glacier (Greenland). 1868. 2F. MMA

—all through the same sharply focused, utterly objective lens. When Gardner published his definitive *Photographic Sketch Book of the War* in 1865, no less than forty-four of the one hundred photographs were by O'Sullivan.

In 1867 O'Sullivan left Gardner to join Clarence King's Fortieth Parallel Survey.[142] The company O'Sullivan now found himself in was as congenial as the terrain was inhospitable. King, at just twenty-five, was fresh from a year in New York, where he was a charter member of a Ruskinian group, the Society for Truth in Art. He was a connoisseur as well as an outdoorsman, considering himself both a geologist and a poet. And since he had worked with C. E. Watkins in Yosemite on the Whitney Survey of 1866, he was aware of the camera's potential and sought to include photography as an artistic as well as a scientific addition to his survey.

eloquent photographs made by John Dunmore (Fig. 130), some of which were used by Bradford as studies for paintings, were made in extreme cold, but Bradford's ship provided shelter as well as the amenities of civilized life, making for working conditions substantially different from those O'Sullivan encountered in the western wilderness. In contrast, O'Sullivan surmounted the hardships of the Civil War battlefields, the remote mountain ranges, deserts, and canyons of the Great Basin, and the tropical jungles of Panama. His western work demonstrated that the obstacles of uncharted terrain could be overcome, but of far more lasting importance was his conviction that barren subjects could often yield photographic images of extraordinary impact and formal beauty.

The static, meticulous compositions that give O'Sullivan's work such a classic flavor provide no hint of the toll making them took on the photographer. Returning from the Southwest for the last time, in 1875, he already had symptoms of the tuberculosis to which he would succumb seven years later. Little is known of his activities in the late

seventies, and few photographs survive from these last years. On the death of his friend L. E. Walker, photographer to the Treasury Department, O'Sullivan applied for the position, submitting an impressive list of recommendations headed by Brady's.[141] In 1880 he was awarded the post but five months later resigned and returned to his father's home in New Brighton, Staten Island, where he died on 14 January 1882.

In 1862, when Alexander Gardner left Brady's employ and opened his own gallery in Washington, O'Sullivan went with him. For the remainder of the Civil War he worked for Gardner and was present on many of the major battlefields from Second Manassas to Appomattox. O'Sullivan built his reputation as a photographer of the Civil War, which led to his development of an esthetic appropriate to the scale and impersonality of "modern" warfare. He recorded the awesome new firepower in images of the destroyed forts, the new weapon of engineering in pictures of the pontoon bridges spanning the Rappahannock River (Fig. 131), and the dead only hours after they had fallen at Gettysburg (Fig. 132)

131. T. H. O'Sullivan. Jericho Mills from North Bank of North Anna, Va., May, 1864. No. 727. S. MMA

The 8 May 1867 issue of *The New York Times* included a brief article announcing King's departure from New York for California on the first federal exploring party in the West after the Civil War. O'Sullivan was listed as the survey's photographer and the report asserted that:

The section to be surveyed is a belt of land about 100 miles wide, near the 40th parallel of latitude, between the 120th and the 105th degrees of longitude, or in other words, from Virginia City (Nevada) to Denver City, a stretch of 800 or 900 miles in length. This strip includes the proposed route of the Central Pacific Railroad, on which the work is progressing so rapidly, and it is the object of the Government to ascertain all the characteristics of the region which is thus to be traversed.... The minerals, flora and the fauna of the country, and its agricultural capacity are likewise to be studied and reported on. In fact, all the work of nature in that wild and unknown region is to be scanned by shrewd and highly-educated observers.

132. T. H. O'Sullivan. On the Battle-Field of Gettysburg. No. 257. 1864. S. MMA

Starting out from Sacramento in early July, the group crossed the Sierra Nevada via the Donner Pass to the mining towns of western Nevada. At Virginia City O'Sullivan descended into the shafts of the Comstock Lode to photograph with an improvised magnesium flash apparatus. Taken hundreds of feet below sunlight, these are the earliest known photographs of mine interiors. O'Sullivan intuitively seized upon the structure of this subterranean world with its imprisoned population working within the stark geometry of the shafts. Few photographers since have conveyed so intensely the claustrophobic existence underground. (Fig. 133). His image of miners waiting to descend the Curtis Shaft of the Savage Mine (Fig. 134) contains a sense of finality reminiscent of a Last Judgment while his image of a mine cave-in (Gould and Curry Mine) (Fig. 135) is simultaneously a factual record of the disaster and a strikingly abstract composition.

Continuing eastward, the survey reached the Truckee River, down which a number of the party,

133. Top, left: T. H. O'Sullivan. Interior of the Savage Mine (Nevada). 1868. ENLARGED S. NA

134. Top, Right: T. H. O'Sullivan. Savage Mine, Curtis Shaft (Nevada). 1868. F. NA

135. Above: T. H. O'Sullivan. Interior of the Gould and Curry Mine (Nevada). 1868. F. NA

136. T. H. O'Sullivan. Pyramid Lake (Nevada). 1868. F. NA

137. T. H. O'Sullivan. "Karnak," Montezuma Range (Nevada). 1868. F. NA

including O'Sullivan, decided to make the first descent by boat into Pyramid Lake. The rapids were treacherous, and it was only thanks to O'Sullivan's strength as a swimmer that the party escaped destruction. The saline and desolate lake held great interest for the photographer as well as the geologists. O'Sullivan recorded the tufa formations of the dominant, pyramidal island (Pl. 36) and the organic shapes of the volcanic rocks protruding from the water (Pl. 40) in pictures that function as both objective geological specimens and fantasy landscapes (Fig. 136).

The entire party then entered the alkali and sagebrush wasteland of the Humboldt Sink, where the vertical and sharply fractured rock strata made the ridges almost inaccessible. Obviously challenged by the beauty and structure of these formations, O'Sullivan managed to photograph them on several occasions (Pl. 37). An image recording the "Karnak" region of the Montezuma Range (Fig. 137)—and including a camera balanced on a splinter of rock to provide scale—functions secondarily as a symbol of the struggle between the photographer with his delicate apparatus and his rugged subject.

Commenting on the Humboldt and neighboring Carson sinks, O'Sullivan observed that "it was a pretty location to work in, and viewing there was as pleasant work as could be desired; the only drawback was an unlimited number of the most voracious and particularly poisonous mosquitoes that we met with during our entire trip. Add to this the entire impossibility to save one's precious body from frequent attacks of that most enervating of all fevers, known as the 'mountain ail' and you will see why we did not work up more of that country."[143]

O'Sullivan's photographs convey the pleasure he clearly derived from exploring and recording the unadorned beauty of these remote landscapes. Unlike Watkins and Muybridge, who returned repeatedly to the comparative Eden of Yosemite Valley to sift out the ideal time, day, and season for each view, he was constantly on the move, rarely taking more than a few photographs of any given subject and remaining for the most part in areas that have never been considered either worthy or in need of national park status.

Between 1867 and 1869 the King Survey worked eastward, charting the Ruby, Wahsatch, and Uinta mountains and the Great Salt Lake basin. Early in 1868 O'Sullivan visited Alkaline Lake in the Nevada waste, meticulously placing his companions in the fore- and middle ground to lead the eye gradually into this eloquently empty landscape (Pl. 39). At a hot spring in the Ruby Valley desert he posed a figure gazing at its reflection in the brackish water to produce one of his most desolate yet poetic images (Fig. 138). South of the Carson Sink, using a mule-drawn ambulance to transport sufficient water for a darkroom, O'Sullivan photographed the shifting dunes near Sand Springs, Nevada (Pl. 35).

138. T. H. O'Sullivan. Hot Springs, Ruby Valley, Nevada. 1868. F. NA

In October 1868, with a small party led by King, O'Sullivan reached the spectacular Shoshone Falls on the Snake River. They pitched camp at the water's edge directly upstream, and from here O'Sullivan photographed the delicately carved gorge receding beyond the brink of the falls, which remains invisible, its presence only suggested by a transparent curtain of mist (Pl. 42). Against this carefully composed backdrop of natural beauty he contrasts, in center foreground, members of the party taking survey measurements. This deliberate emphasis on one of the central purposes of the expedition—the measuring and reducing to charts and mathematical tables of these vast panoramas—underlines his attitude toward his own instrument, the camera. O'Sullivan used his camera much as the surveyors did their levels, telescopes, and tripods, to record his surroundings as objectively and factually as possible. One senses that for O'Sullivan a photograph was equally an image chosen and organized by the artist and a specimen of preexisting physical fact recorded by the technician. The perfectly balanced tension between these subjective and objective concerns is a central characteristic of his work.

In 1869 O'Sullivan was first in Salt Lake City and then in southern Wyoming and northern Colorado, where he photographed the Green River and Flaming Gorge (Pls. 51, 52). In September, King's expedition concluded, he returned to New York to become the photographer to the Darien Survey. Under the command of Lt. Comdr. Thomas O. Selfridge, the expedition was to determine possible routes for a canal through the Isthmus of Panama. O'Sullivan managed to photograph in the humid climate and dense undergrowth, but clearly the terrain did not lend itself to his esthetic concerns (Fig. 139). The dense foliage filtered the bold lighting he preferred, and the exotic vegetation did not present the range of formal opportunities which he had found in the rock and sand of the western landscape.

It is not surprising, then, that in 1871 he was

139. T. H. O'Sullivan. Panama. 1868. F. IMP/GEH

again in the West, this time with the Geological Surveys West of the One Hundredth Meridian, under the command of Lt. George M. Wheeler of the Corps of Engineers.[144] In contrast to King, Wheeler was a West Pointer and a career officer with little interest in the arts or the philosophical controversies that surrounded contemporary science. His survey proposal downplayed the relevance of geological and natural history research and stressed the importance of topographical mapping and the locating of natural resources, with an eye toward military access to the territory of Nevada, Utah, Arizona, and New Mexico. Photography for Wheeler was not so much a scientific

tool as it was a means of publicizing the survey's accomplishments in the hope of persuading Congress to fund military, rather than civilian, expeditions in the future. While O'Sullivan had been working under geologists on the King Survey, his position with Wheeler was increasingly independent. In fact, recognizing O'Sullivan's experience and leadership ability, Wheeler repeatedly appointed him "executive-in-charge" of portions of the expedition.

By late spring 1871, Wheeler's party had assembled at Ft. Halleck, Nevada, and in the first week of May the expedition headed south, passing through Owens Valley, in July crossing Death Valley—where the temperature rose so high that the photographic chemicals boiled—and traveling on to Camp Mojave on the lower Colorado River. From here a portion of the party set out in four flat-bottomed boats to attempt an ascent of the Colorado through the Grand Canyon to the mouth of Diamond Creek (Figs. 140, 141). Wheeler defended the ascent—admittedly of little scientific value—as necessary to determine the limits of practical navigation. With O'Sullivan in command of the second boat, which he christened "The Picture," they rowed, towed, and portaged up 260 miles of river through some of the most treacherous rapids in the world, rejoining the main party thirty-one days later, having lost much of their equipment and nearly succumbed to starvation. "Mr. O'Sullivan," Wheeler noted later in his report, "in the face of all obstacles, made negatives at all available points, some of which were saved, but the principal ones of the collection were ruined during transportation from Prescott, Arizona."[145]

Despite this loss, the exact extent of which is unknown, O'Sullivan's surviving views of the can-

141. T. H. O'Sullivan. Snug Harbor, Black Cañon. Halt for the Night. No. 5. 1871. s. LC

142. T. H. O'Sullivan. Cottonwood Lake. Wahsatch Mountains (Utah). 1868. F. NA

yons of the Colorado are among his finest. So painstakingly composed are his Black Canyon images of water, sand, and rock, modulated by the stark Arizona light, that were it not for the notebook entries of the party's geologist, G. K. Gilbert,[146] one would never guess the exhausting conditions under which they were realized. The view from Camp 8, Looking Above (Pl. 57)—with O'Sullivan's boat in the foreground containing a hunched figure, perhaps Gilbert recording the day's events—is one of O'Sullivan's most evocative. Surrounded by rugged canyon walls and with the fast-flowing Colorado blurred to a metallic sheen by the slow exposure, man is presented as cerebral and reflective in the face of nature, an unobtrusive presence rather than a vehicle for dramatizing a confrontation with the sublime. This concept of a sympathetic relationship between man and nature is closer in spirit to Clarence King's philosophy than to Wheeler's vision of man in continual opposition to his environment. Several years earlier O'Sullivan had photographed another landscape containing a boat and a contemplative figure in the foreground (Fig. 142). The figure in the earlier photograph is very probably the photographer himself, scrutinizing a freshly developed glass-plate negative. In this rare portrait of the artist, O'Sullivan presents himself surrounded by actual wilderness but entranced by its replica recorded in his photograph.

In April 1872 O'Sullivan was temporarily transferred with his consent, to Utah, where King was leading an expedition near the route of the recently completed Central Pacific Railroad, but the only visual evidence of the foray is a handful of stereographic views. He remained with King for the rest of the year and revisited the magnificent valley of the Green River. Beginning in June, the Phil-

144. T. H. O'Sullivan. Aboriginal Life among the Navajo Indians (New Mexico). No. 26. 1873. s. LC

adelphian William Bell replaced O'Sullivan with Wheeler's expedition and worked primarily in the Grand Canyon (Fig. 143). If O'Sullivan's sensibility was more akin to King's, Bell's esthetic was well suited to the role Wheeler had intended for photography. Bell preferred dramatic viewpoints and extreme spatial juxtapositions; figures, when they appeared, served to illustrate man's awe of nature.

In 1873 O'Sullivan led an independent expedition for Wheeler, visiting the Zuni and Magia pueblos and the Canyon de Chelly, with its remnants of a cliff-dwelling culture nestled beneath the towering rocks (Pls. 62, 63). Little is known of O'Sullivan in 1874/1875 except that he was once again in the Southwest photographing Indians. Unlike many ethnographic photographers, who posed Indians either in the studio or against neutral backgrounds outdoors, O'Sullivan allowed his subjects to command their environment. The resulting pictures are remarkably objective (Figs. 144, 145). Just as the Apache scouts in his view of Apache Lake of 1873 (Pl. 60) are among the few truly threatening and unromanticized images of the western Indian, the 1874/1875 photographs convey a sincere interest and a respect untinged by the sentimentality that colors so many later photographs of the same subject. After the completion of the 1875 Wheeler Expedition, O'Sullivan returned to the East, leaving forever the land and the people he had spent such energy recording.

At first the abrupt change from O'Sullivan's dramatic coverage of the Civil War to the relative emptiness of his western landscapes appears a complete one. However, the style he had arrived at by 1863 in his Gettysburg photographs, with their insistence on static visual evidence, had a direct application to landscape—particularly to

143. Wm. Bell. Devil's Anvil, Sheavwitz Crossing (Arizona). 1872. s. ALB

145. T. H. O'Sullivan. Types of Mojave Indians (Arizona). No. 5. 1871. s. LC

146. T. H. O'Sullivan. "A Harvest of Death," Gettysburg, 1863. F. IMP/GEH

147. T. H. O'Sullivan. Metamorphic Limestone, W. Humboldt Mountains. 1868. I. AGS

landscape seen through the eyes of the geologist.

While Brady was primarily interested in recording the historic personalities and events of the war, Alexander Gardner, O'Sullivan's later employer, was aware of what Walt Whitman had reported in *Specimen Days*—that war's ultimate truth could only be found in its anonymous details.[147] Referring to O'Sullivan's A Harvest of Death (Fig. 146), Gardner observed that "such a picture . . . shows the blank horror and reality of war, in opposition to its pageantry. Here are the dreadful details!"[148] To convey something of the vast, impersonal forces that had determined the battle's outcome, O'Sullivan turned to the evidence left behind. The result was a landscape of war's aftermath.

The decision to join Clarence King's survey was crucial to the development of O'Sullivan's style, for the demands of geological photography provided an ideal transition from those of journalism to the treatment of pure landscape. Just as the bodies of the dead, receding into the distance, outline the course of the recent struggle, the rock formations he was soon recording were the visible evidence of immense forces active in the distant past (Fig. 147). From his journalistic emphasis on "the decisive moment," which had nearly cost him his life at Bull Run, to the dead on the field at Gettysburg, which provided the visible record of human history, to the underlying form and structure of the landscape itself, which spoke in terms of geological time, O'Sullivan expanded his notion of what could provide the subject for a photograph. This question of time and how it could be visually recorded became a central concern and the unstated subject of images such as Rock Carved by Drifting Sand (Pl. 58). In what is perhaps his masterpiece of the last years, the Ancient Ruins in the Canyon de Chelly (Pl. 62), the present—in the form of the tiny figures standing amidst the ruins—the historic past, and the timeless pace of erosion are all combined in relative proportion in a single photographic image.

O'Sullivan quickly learned that an "empty" landscape could have great geological significance, but more important, he perceived that an "empty" landscape did not necessarily result in an esthetically empty photograph. In his hands the scientific recording of geological structure led logically to an increased concern for the abstract structuring of the resulting two-dimensional image. This mutually enhancing relationship between factual, geological information and purely formal, visual information resulted in photographs that are powerfully abstract without being gratuitous. In contrast to the work of later, more consciously modernist nature photographers, the best of the survey photographs convey a pragmatic sense of purpose in addition to radical visual experimentation.

O'Sullivan's landscape work is clearly distinguishable from that of his contemporaries, not only in terms of the geographic areas where he worked, but of the style he established as early as 1868. He composed his photographs with great care, selecting the point of view and lighting to reproduce a given subject as concretely and comprehensibly as possible. His photographs convey an almost obsessive determination to transfer with equal emphasis every detail of the world before his lens to the confined, two-dimensional surface of the glass plate—an ambition perfectly suited to the remarkable power of the wet-collodion process to resolve detail.

O'Sullivan pursued this approach to what he considered photographic truth with characteristic consistency and purity. His image of the Historic Spanish Record of the Conquest, South Side of Inscription Rock (Pl. 59) includes a ruler propped on a yucca spine to verify the exact scale of the carving, thus adding mathematical evidence of its actual size to the purely visual record. This desire to calibrate the physical dimensions of the subject, here so strikingly overt, is present in even his most panoramic compositions, where the eye is led into depth gradually and systematically to avoid any dislocating break from the immediate foreground to the horizon. Just as the overriding technological accomplishment of the age—the completion of the transcontinental railroad in 1869—subjugated what had been incomprehensible space to the measured rhythm of its evenly spaced ties, the camera in O'Sullivan's hands probed even the most awesome landscape for its underlying structure.

William Bell's photographs for Wheeler in 1872, some of which have been confused with O'Sullivan's, provide an instructive comparison. In direct contrast to O'Sullivan's style, Bell preferred vertical formats, diagonal compositions, and calculatedly disruptive jumps in scale and distance. His

148. Wm. Bell. Cañon of Kanab Wash, Colorado River, Looking South (Arizona). 1872. F. BPL

149. Wm. Bell. Looking South into the Grand Cañon, Colorado River (Arizona). 1872. F. BPL

Canyon of Kanab Wash, Colorado River, Looking South (Fig. 148) and Looking South into the Grand Canyon, Colorado River (Fig. 149), dramatize the natural settings through extreme camera angles and a consciously ambiguous treatment of receding space. Confronted with a similar landscape, O'Sullivan strove to convey its underlying formal and geological order. To photograph the Canyon of the Colorado River near the mouth of the San Juan River (Pl. 53), he maneuvered his camera to the point where the maze of cliffs zigzag, layer by layer, with an ordered rhythm into depth and the sun's reflection off the smooth water at the San Juan's mouth registers as a white crescent at the exact center of the composition. Recording the rock formations of the Green River Valley, he composed the spectacular strata into a progression of tightly intersecting arcs softened by the overall, pointillistic dots of scrub vegetation (Pl. 52). On the rare occasions when he introduced an abrupt spatial recession, as in his view of the Green River near Flaming Gorge (Pl. 51), the foreground rocks are related unambiguously to the landscape beyond, the intervening distance clearly measured by the connecting curve of the river.

These characteristics did not lend themselves to the demands of the stereoscopic viewer with its preference for verticality and dramatic, three-dimensional spatial relationships. Consequently,

while O'Sullivan's stereo views are often impressive, they are frequently cropped versions of compositions conceived as horizontal, single-image prints. This is hardly surprising given his concern for the surface continuity of the photograph as an object, in contrast to the all-encompassing spatial illusion of the stereoscopic image.

O'Sullivan's expression of extreme scale without spatial disruption is comparable in many ways to Watkins's work in Yosemite in 1866, which was also influenced by Clarence King. While frequently including the human figure in his compositions, O'Sullivan often cropped it radically, as in the case of the anonymous human presence in Geyser Mouth, Ruby Valley, Nevada Territory (Pl. 41). The three tiny white tents in Canyon de Chelly,

Walls of the Grand Canyon (Pl. 63) produce a brilliant counterpoint to the massive black slabs of rock towering above them. The single tree, silhouetted in shadow at the foot of Explorer's Column, Canyon de Chelly (Fig. 150) provides a comprehensible module with which to gauge the height of that immense geological wonder. In contrast, two images made from negatives from which no contemporary prints are recorded demonstrate the monumental photographic presence O'Sullivan could extract from the close-up of a single, isolated object (Figs. 151, 152).

O'Sullivan took great care to relate the internal forms of his images to the rectangular format of the photographic plate. Similarly, his treatment of light is primarily structural rather than dramatic.

150. T. H. O'Sullivan. Distant View of Explorers Column, Cañon de Chelle (Arizona). 1873. s. LC

NEW MEXICO SERIES.

EXPEDITION OF 1873.

1st Lieut. GEO. M. WHEELER, Corps of Eng'rs, Com'dg.

T. H. O'Sullivan, Phot.

No. 14.—Distant View of Explorers Column, Cañon de Chelle, about 900 ft. in height.

Several of the Black Canyon photographs are pure studies in light and shadow, which record—as in Looking Below, Near Camp 7 (Pl. 56)—the vast range of tones from full sunlight falling on rock and water to the near-black shadow cast by the cliff at the right, in which O'Sullivan's boat, "The Picture," is barely discernible. In this, as in all his pictures, the flat white, crisply defined negative shape of the sky is a carefully articulated element of the total composition. The sky in the head-on view of Vermillion Creek Canyon (Pl. 55) carries a visual emphasis equal to that of the rocks themselves.

O'Sullivan's views are among the least picturesque of all western landscape photographs. This is partially explained by his relative isolation from a critical milieu based on the esthetics of painting and on his financial dependence on meeting the needs of the government surveys rather than those of a marketplace where photographers were in competition with painters. It is primarily, however, the result of an uncompromisingly photographic vision, which was reinforced rather than diluted by the requirements of geological recording.

This is nowhere more apparent than in utterly unprepossessing images such as City of Rocks, Idaho (Pl. 44), which register as intricately textured surfaces before any specific forms are discernible. For a parallel to this treatment of landscape one must look to the paintings of O'Sullivan's contemporary Cézanne, where foreground and depth are woven into a single, unbroken surface of brush strokes. Through the camera's ability to capture in sharp focus objects both near and far, O'Sullivan recorded the close-up and distant structure of rock and vegetation with such intensity that they fuse into a single visual whole.

O'Sullivan's photographs reveal a love for the land as fundamental as his love for photography. Nevertheless, his goal was one of exploration rather than conservation. One source of the vigor of his style is the sense of discovery it conveys. There is no trace in his work of an escape to the wilderness from an alienating urban environment. The modernity his images hold for us is not the result of our awareness that much of what he photographed has been destroyed or become endangered but derives from the austerity of his preferred subjects and the intense esthetic consciousness of his vision.

PLATE 35. T. H. O'SULLIVAN. DESERT SAND HILLS NEAR SINK OF CARSON (NEVADA). 1868. F. LC

PLATE 36. T. H. O'SULLIVAN. TUFA ROCKS, PYRAMID LAKE (NEVADA). 1868. F. NA

PLATE 37. T. H. O'SULLIVAN. VOLCANIC RIDGE, TRINITY MOUNTAINS (NEVADA). 1868. F. NA

PLATE 38. T. H. O'SULLIVAN. RUBY VALLEY (NEVADA). 1868. F. AGS

PLATE 39. T. H. O'SULLIVAN. ALKALINE LAKE, CARSON DESERT (NEVADA). 1868. F. AGS

PLATE 40. T. H. O'SULLIVAN. ROCK FORMATIONS, PYRAMID LAKE (NEVADA). 1868. F. MIT

PLATE 41. T. H. O'SULLIVAN. GEYSER MOUTH, RUBY VALLEY (NEVADA). 1868. F. AGS

PLATE 42. T. H. O'SULLIVAN. SHOSHONE FALLS (IDAHO). 1868. F. AGS

PLATE 43. T. H. O'SULLIVAN. CANON OF THE SNAKE RIVER (IDAHO). 1868. F. AGS

PLATE 44. T. H. O'SULLIVAN. CITY OF ROCKS—GRANITE (IDAHO). 1867. F. LC

PLATE 45. T. H. O'SULLIVAN. UNIDENTIFIED. ABOUT 1868. F. AGS

PLATE 46. T. H. O'SULLIVAN. VOLCANIC ISLANDS, MONO LAKE, CALIFORNIA. ABOUT 1868. F. LC

PLATE 47. T. H. O'SULLIVAN. SALT LAKE CITY. ABOUT 1868. F. AGS

PLATE 48. T. H. O'SULLIVAN. PROVO FALLS, PROVO CANON, WAHSATCH MOUNTAINS (UTAH). ABOUT 1868. F. AGS

PLATE 49. T. H. O'SULLIVAN. LIMESTONE CANON NEAR FORT RUBY (NEVADA). ABOUT 1868. F. NA

PLATE 50. T. H. O'SULLIVAN. MOUNT AGASSIZ (UTAH). ABOUT 1868. F. NA

PLATE 51. T. H. O'SULLIVAN. GREEN RIVER NEAR FLAMING GORGE (COLORADO). ABOUT 1868. F. LC

PLATE 52. T. H. O'SULLIVAN. GREEN RIVER (COLORADO). ABOUT 1868. F. LC

PLATE 53. T. H. O'SULLIVAN. CANON OF THE COLORADO RIVER, NEAR MOUTH OF SAN JUAN RIVER, ARIZONA. 1873. F. BPL

PLATE 54. T. H. O'SULLIVAN. WALLS OF THE GRAND
CANON, COLORADO RIVER, ARIZONA. 1871.
F. BPL

PLATE 55. T. H. O'SULLIVAN. UNIDENTIFIED (VERMILLION CREEK CANON, UTAH). ABOUT 1868. F. LC

PLATE 56. T. H. O'SULLIVAN. BLACK CANON, COLORADO RIVER, LOOKING BELOW, NEAR CAMP 7 (ARIZONA). 1871. F. BPL

PLATE 57. T. H. O'SULLIVAN. BLACK CANON, COLORADO RIVER, FROM CAMP 8, LOOKING ABOVE (ARIZONA). 1871. F. BPL

PLATE 58. T. H. O'SULLIVAN. ROCK CARVED BY DRIFTING SAND, BELOW FORTIFICATION ROCK, ARIZONA. 1871. F. LC

PLATE 59. T. H. O'SULLIVAN. HISTORIC SPANISH RECORD OF THE CONQUEST, SOUTH SIDE OF INSCRIPTION ROCK, NEW MEXICO. 1873. F. LC

PLATE 60. T. H. O'SULLIVAN. APACHE LAKE, SIERRA BLANCA RANGE, ARIZONA. 1873. F. SW

PLATE 61. T. H. O'SULLIVAN. VIEW ON APACHE LAKE,
SIERRA BLANCA RANGE, ARIZONA. 1873. F. SW

PLATE 62.
T. H. O'SULLIVAN. ANCIENT RUINS IN
THE CANON DE CHELLE, N. M.
(TERRITORY). 1873. F. BPL

PLATE 63. T. H. O'SULLIVAN. CANON DE CHELLE, WALLS OF THE GRAND CANON ABOUT 1200 FEET IN HEIGHT, 1873. F. P

PLATE 64. T. H. O'SULLIVAN. UNIDENTIFIED. 1870–1873. F. NA

Eadweard J. Muybridge

1830-1904

153. E. J. Muybridge ("Helios"). A View from Fort Point, San Francisco. No. 438. About 1869. s. MMA

Muybridge was justifiably celebrated as a landscape photographer for his series of mammoth-plate Yosemite views made in 1872 and offered for sale by Bradley and Rulofson in 1873. These fifty-one ambitious photographs were made in direct competition with C. E. Watkins's equally acclaimed views of 1861–1866 (Pls. 1-24, 26). Muybridge is most often remembered for his photographs of humans and animals in motion, and his impressive Yosemite views suggest that prior to the experiments in motion he was primarily a landscape photographer. Such was not the case, however, for while Muybridge was a pioneer in outdoor work, he was attracted to the wilderness for only a brief time in a long career devoted mainly to other types of photography.

Relatively little is known of Muybridge's work before 1873. In that year Bradley and Rulofson, one of San Francisco's most important portrait studios and galleries of photography, published an extensive collection of his photographs with an accompanying catalogue.[149] The catalogue lists approximately 1400 views from 5½-by-8½-inch plates, 100 views from five-by-seven-inch plates, and fifty-one views from mammoth plates. Unfortunately the photographs are not identified by date, but a rough chronology can be deduced from the dates and numbers on the stereoscopic photographs. The lowest numbers, from 200 upward, appear on scenes from around San Francisco. The earliest of these date from 1866/1867, judging from the costumes, architecture, and the prevalence of military subjects; a view of the aftermath of the earthquake of 2 October 1868 falls in the mid-400s. The highest numbers are on pictures of events that took place about the time the catalogue appeared—Muy-

154.
E. J. Muybridge.
Panorama of San Francisco
in Six Parts. About 1869. H. UCB

OPPOSITE PAGE:

155.
E. J. Muybridge.
Mission Bay from Rincon Hill.
No. 355. About 1868. S. MMA

156.
E. J. Muybridge.
Wahsatch Mountains, from
the Weber River (Utah).
No. 760. About 1870. S. MMA

bridge's 1872 trip to Yosemite and the Modoc War of the same year. These later pictures are numbered in the 1500s and 1600s. The photographs published by Bradley and Rulofson illustrate Muybridge's style prior to 1873, before photographing motion became so important to him.

Muybridge was born in Kingston-on-Thames in England but by 1855 lived in San Francisco, where he was proprietor of a bookstore specializing in illustrated books.[150] He spent his early years photographing daily life in California, chronicling the development of industry (Fig. 153) and agriculture in the state. Among his favorite subjects was the city of San Francisco (Fig. 154), which he endlessly studied for its architecture and ambience. He was constantly attracted to the waterfront and shipping activity (Figs. 5, 155, 160) both in the city and in the small harbors up the coast and even photographed a series of lighthouses. Muybridge also photogaphed missions, vineyards, wineries, and railroads and made a few photographs of Indians. His brothers apparently tended the store while he traveled around the state selling books to newly prosperous gentlemen. He came to know the geography of California well and soon realized people's desire to have pictures of it. Eventually he traveled to Alaska (Pls. 65-67), the Farallone Islands, and Vancouver Island, recording the path of civilization to those areas. By 1873 he had spent much time photographing outdoors and was a masterful picture journalist; he even captioned one of his series "Photographic *Illustrations* [sic] of the Pacific Coast." His photographs include people wherever possible and are always well composed. However, his published work includes few photographs of landscape for its own sake, apart from views made in Yosemite in 1867 and 1872. Muybridge documented the route of the new Central Pacific Railroad about 1870, and a fine series of landscape views were the results of the excursion. Some of these suggest his success at capturing clouds on the same negative as landscape without having to resort to printing from two negatives (Fig. 156).

157. Francis Frith. Unidentified village. No. 91. Dated Nov. 15, 1859. s. MMA

158. G. W. Wilson. Edinburgh—Princes Street Looking West (instantaneous). No.185. About 1860. s. MMA

159. Francis Bedford. Lydstep—The Natural Arch, South Wales. No. 2294. About 1865. s. MMA

Muybridge had been injured in a stagecoach accident in 1860 and had gone back to England for medical treatment. When he returned to California he had the skills of a professional photographer, and his early work suggests the influence of the masters of British topographical photography—Francis Frith (Figs. 21, 157), G. W. Wilson (Fig. 158), and Francis Bedford (Fig. 159). He must have seen many of these photographs, for his own choice of subjects, style of composition, and technical sophistication echo the Englishmen's work (Fig. 160). Frith, Wilson, and Bedford were essentially landscape photographers, but they presented the land in terms of man's civilizing effects on it. The interrelationship between man and nature became a guiding principle for Muybridge as well, and he placed figures in his landscapes with a consummate judgment rarely equaled in America in his time (Fig. 161).

Muybridge's first copyrighted photographs of wilderness landscape were a series of Yosemite views registered by the photographer in 1868.[151] He used Silas Sellek's Gallery of Photographic Art as his address and signed himself "Helios" (Figs. 45, 113, Pls. 65, 68) in the 1867 negatives. He used his own name on the labels, however, which suggests that "Helios" was not merely a pseudonym. The signature was conceivably a protection against plagiarism—an issue raised when Thomas Houseworth, the San Francisco optician and photograph dealer, received the highest award for landscape at the 1867 Paris International Exposition. The landscape views Houseworth submitted were actually by other California photographers, including Watkins and Weed, and perhaps even Muybridge. The photographs Houseworth exhibited earned the highest praise from the foreign press as well as from the exposition jury; however, those photographs from Houseworth's catalogue chronicling the advance of civilization in the West received no honors. The rebuff was hardly an encouragement to Muybridge, whose specialty was documenting the California way of life. Also overlooked by the

160. E. J. Muybridge. Panorama, from Rincon Hill. About 1869. s. MMA

162. E. J. Muybridge's advertisement in the endpapers of John S. Hittel's *Yosemite: Its Wonders and Its Beauties,* 1868. sw

exposition jurors were photographs of the dramatic efforts to cut the Central Pacific Railroad through the Sierra Nevada—many of the views by A. A. Hart (Figs. 60, 61).

Pure landscape, particularly that of Yosemite, had come into extraordinary prominence, and it was natural that Muybridge visited and photographed the newly established park, making negatives in the summer of 1867 which were published in 1868 (Fig. 162).[152] The "Helios" signature clearly distinguished his work from Watkins's and Weed's and hindered its being pirated by publishers.

Muybridge made another self-conscious effort to identify his own Yosemite photographs by artfully manipulating—even stylizing—his points of view, as in Vernal Falls (Cataract of Diamonds) (Fig. 113). The rocks loom in the foreground with a blur of water rushing behind them. The point of view understates the 350-foot fall so that it looks smaller than in Watkins's view of 1861 (Fig. 112). Muybridge emphasized the raging force of the water and heightened the contrast between the sinuous stream in the middle ground and the staid granite before it. Watkins, on the other hand, had created a composition of classical serenity in which the main falls descends to the foreground, suggesting the harmony of nature. Muybridge created receding space in the ribbon of water leading back to the falls, while Watkins designed a network of surface geometry; Muybridge's photograph is painterly in contrast to the sharp-focus precision of Watkins's.

Muybridge's Yosemite photographs of 1867 at-

161. E. J. Muybridge. Truckee River, near the Third Crossing. No. 736. About 1870. s. P

his cloud effects which Watkins was later to imitate.

Another striking quality of the 1867 series is Muybridge's sensitivity to the direction and degree of light; he deliberately photographed at times of the day when the sun gave its deepest shadows and brightest highlights. Watkins's 1861 stereos show a similar concern, but by 1866 he had rephotographed many motifs with flat light to minimize the dramatic effect. Muybridge's view of Loya (Sentinel Rock) (Fig. 166) is divided almost diagonally between the dark foreground and the brightly lit background, and another view of the same subject shows it in a very raking light. Po-ho-no (Bridal Veil) is treated with a nearly Rembrandtesque spotlight effect on the falls itself. The Indians named the place To-Coy-Ae ("shade to Indian baby basket"), an effect in nature that Muybridge captured in his photograph (Pl. 69).[154] To-Coy-Ae

164. E. J. Muybridge.
Base of Upper
Yosemite Falls.
1867. H. UCB

tempt to depict the extremes of nature rather than the norms. He photographed Yosemite Falls (Fig. 163) with a necklace of clouds and a raking shadow in the distance, a view in which the Merced River occupies the entire foreground as though the camera were mounted in it. Similarly, the view of the Upper Yosemite Falls from the Yosemite Cave (Fig. 164) presents an unexpected, romanticized point of view.

Muybridge's 1867 photographs are also remarkable for their cloud effects, which were printed from separate negatives, since wet-collodion plates were so sensitive to blue light that the sky was inevitably overexposed. Muybridge later devised a method for reducing the amount of light striking the plate in the blue area. He called it the "sky shade" (Fig. 165) and described its operation in a letter to E. L. Wilson, editor of *The Philadelphia Photographer*.[153] Muybridge gained a reputation for

163. E. J. Muybridge.
Yo-Sem-i-te Falls
(Large Grizzly
Bear). 1867. H. UCB

(North Dome) appears to be spotlighted in contrast to the vast expanse of shadow extending across the valley and up half the mountain.

Also in 1868 Muybridge applied for copyright on a series of photographs made in Alaska (Pls. 65-67), where he traveled under the sponsorship of the controversial General William Halleck, presumably during the summer.[155] In the photographs he made on the journey his choice of unusual points of view is again the dominant artistic element. Indeed, many of the pictures could not have been taken without Muybridge's deliberately seeking out-of-the-way vantage points; he photographed Sitka, Fort Wrangle, and Fort Tongass from across nearby bodies of water. Those remote towns sometimes had little to distinguish them, and Muybridge cleverly solved the problem by transforming townscape into almost pure landscape. His photographs convey the tenuous hold these outposts of civilization had on the land. Even Sitka, which in fact had some architecture to photograph, is rendered in one view as a sliver on the horizon with a vast expanse of marsh grass in the foreground, and in another view the city hovers on the horizon like a backdrop on a stage. Ethnological subjects, too, are treated as almost pure landscapes in views like one of the Indian compound at Fort Wrangle (Pl. 66); the Indians, who had been transported from their village, are subordinated to the tangle of leaves, grasses, and brush that occupies three-quarters of the image.

In their catalogue Bradley and Rulofson referred to Muybridge as "employed during several years by the U.S. Government in the production of the numerous views upon this coast required by the Treasury and War Departments."[156] It is unlikely that Muybridge was employed by the government in the same way O'Sullivan, Jackson, Bell, Beaman, and Hillers were—as salaried staff photographers to the various surveys and expeditions. Perhaps Muybridge worked on speculation; he might have been a volunteer, earning room, board, and transportation only, as Jackson did with the Hayden

Survey and as Watkins appears to have done with the Whitney Survey. The government retained the negatives made by its salaried employees, but Muybridge's views of Alaska and Vancouver Island were published under his own name with the imprint of the Cosmopolitan Gallery of Photographic Art. It would not be surprising to find that the government subsidized Muybridge's travel up the Pacific Coast—even to the inaccessible Farallone Islands—and encouraged him to photograph such unlikely subjects as lighthouses for which there was no popular market. In fact, the rarity today of the Pacific Coast photographs suggests that, even after they were offered for sale by Bradley and Rulofson, the views were seldom purchased. Travelers would have bought views of places they had seen, and visitors from the East, the main customers for such photographs, rarely reached Alaska, the Farallones, or even Vancouver Island.

Muybridge visited Yosemite again in the spring and summer of 1872 and made his most significant and last extensive body of landscape photographs. Drama was the foremost quality in Muybridge's esthetic, and he continued to place heavy emphasis on unique points of view to achieve dramatic intensity. The extent to which he would go for unusual vantage points was noted in the *Alta California*, where it was reported that "he had himself lowered by ropes down precipices. . . . He has gone to points where his packers refused to follow him."[157] Actually Muybridge's 1872 Yosemite viewpoints are less visibly stylized, and the remarkable difficulty of some of the camera locations is apparent only when the photographs are carefully studied. Domes from Glacier Point (Pl. 83), a mammoth-plate photograph, contains many of the same compositional elements as To-Coy-Ae (North Dome)—particularly the large shadow in the valley—but the cliffs on either side are less compelling than in the earlier photograph. After a moment one realizes that for the larger work the camera must have been nearly suspended in space.

In 1872 Muybridge was with, among others, Al-

165. Attributed to E. J. Muybridge. Horizontal Sky Shade. About 1867. SU

166. E. J. Muybridge. Loya (Sentinel Rock, Yosemite). 1867. H. UCB

OPPOSITE PAGE:

168. C. E. Watkins. The Half-Dome from Glacier Point (Yosemite). No. 101. 1866. M. SW

169. E. J. Muybridge. The Half Dome (Yosemite). 1867. H. UCB

167. E. J. Muybridge. Rainbow at Piwyack (Yosemite). About 1872. S. IMP/GEH

bert Bierstadt, the landscape painter, and Clarence King, the geologist, whose Fortieth Parallel Survey was coming to an end. Both these men had strong feelings about the esthetics of landscape, which surely influenced Muybridge's thinking. *Alta California* related that he made the Yosemite views in partnership with Bierstadt, receiving suggestions on the points of view from him, and, further, that Muybridge made other views at King's suggestion.[158] Muybridge's esthetic premises had matured significantly since 1867; the 1872 mammoth-plate views and stereos do not represent a full about-face but rather a refinement of sensibility and a modest redirection in the choice of subjects. Bierstadt may have encouraged Muybridge to try new atmospheric effects, which played an important role in Bierstadt's paintings; perhaps this is reflected in photographs such as Rainbow at Piwyack (sic) (Fig. 167) and in photographs of clouds and plants Muybridge called "Yosemite Studies." Bierstadt was also interested in pictures with a heightened sense of space, and it is conceivable that the dominance of spatiality, which replaced Muybridge's earlier concern for light, emerged as a result of Bierstadt's influence.

The *Alta California* related that Clarence King specifically suggested the motif of the ancient glacier channel seen from Panorama Rock, a subject that lacks the dramatic impact Muybridge con-

sistently delivered when working independently. It is possible that King drew Muybridge's attention to the subtle beauty of rock formations and stream beds (Pl. 77) carved by centuries of rushing water. King had earlier influenced both Watkins and O'Sullivan.

The public response to Muybridge's 1872 photographs was overwhelming. The reaction to his first Yosemite views had been highly favorable, and *Alta California* said they surpassed "in artistic excellence, anything that has yet been published in San Francisco."[159] It was clear to all who read these lines that Muybridge was being praised over Watkins. In 1873 Bradley and Rulofson sent Muybridge's photographs to the jurors of the International Exposition in Vienna, and they were awarded

the medal of progress for landscape. This award escalated Muybridge to international prominence previously enjoyed only by C. E. Watkins among American photographers. O'Sullivan's photographs were also submitted to Vienna by Lt. George Wheeler but were barely noticed. Dr. Hermann Vogel, the German correspondent to *The Philadelphia Photographer*, praised Muybridge's views and expressed regret that they were not better known in Berlin since "landscapes of this size are the exception here."[160] Vogel was perhaps the most prominent German photographer, teacher, and theoretician, and his praise reveals the accomplishments of California landscape photographers compared to their European counterparts.

Muybridge's triumph obscured the specifics of

the artistic competition between him and Watkins. Critics failed to recognize the stylistic difference between the two—that they were as different as romanticism and classicism—but rather interpreted Muybridge's work as "progress" to a new level of art. They overlooked Watkins's pioneering mammoth-plate photographs of 1861–1866 (Pls. 1–4, 16), without which Muybridge's similar work might never have existed. Muybridge himself never acknowledged his debt to Watkins (Figs. 45, 51, 168, 169); in all the printed announcements for his Yosemite photographs he claimed the superiority of his own work.

In 1873 Susan Coolidge, who wrote about San Francisco for *Scribner's Monthly*, fueled the competition between Muybridge and Watkins when she

The studies of motion were interrupted by bizarre circumstances in Muybridge's family life that caused him to kill his wife's lover, a crime of which he was acquitted on grounds of justifiable homicide.[163] Even so, Muybridge prudently left San Francisco after the widely publicized trial.

He went to Central America in 1875, and during his first season there his fully developed artistic personality emerged. He had long been a master of photojournalism as well as landscape photography, and in the Central America pictures he drew on both disciplines. The resulting photographs are at the summit of his journalistic career. Most of the photographs record the environment and life of the people: soldiers and natives in the cities, villages, and port towns (Fig. 170). Pure landscape photographs are rare, but those understated images Muybridge made of the densely carpeted rain forests and the fuming latent volcanoes are compelling records. The Central America photographs show that Muybridge was not an artist who limited himself but rather had the ranging versatility and inquisitive temperament of great artists in every medium.[164]

The horse-in-motion experiments of 1872 were expanded into a full-fledged scientific investigation after Muybridge returned from Central America late in 1875. From the summer of 1877 until the spring of 1881, with the assistance of helpers that Stanford provided, Muybridge designed and supervised the construction of an apparatus for photographing all phases of a horse's stride (Fig. 171). By 1878 he had created a device for using twelve cameras and by 1881 had an apparatus for using up to twenty-four.[165]

In 1881 Muybridge went to Europe, where he had the recognition of artists and scientists for his research of motion. He was entertained by Professor E.-J. Marey in Paris and greeted by artists and writers of such international stature as Alexandre Dumas, J. L. Gérôme, and J.-L.-E. Meissonier.[166] Muybridge had the attention of the world upon him for his studies of human and animal motion. He never seriously resumed landscape photography.

wrote: "The Watkins photographs are too well known to require comment; but I should like to mention that Mr. Muybridge, a photographer not so long before the public will exhibit this spring a series of large YO-Semite views, finer and more perfect than any which have ever before been taken.[161] Muybridge's rise to fame was as dramatic as his photographs; Watkins, on the other hand, went bankrupt shortly after the review appeared.

Muybridge's career was also about to change. In 1872 California Governor Leland Stanford wagered a friend that a horse in full gallop had all four of its feet off the ground simultaneously at some point in its stride. Muybridge was commissioned to produce a series of experimental photographs of Stanford's own horse, Occident.[162] The original photographs have apparently not survived, but the experiment was documented in a lithograph by Currier and Ives.

170. E. J. Muybridge. San Isidro, Guatemala. No. 1978. About 1875. s. p

171. E. J. Muybridge. Horse and Rider In Motion. 1878. F. MMA

PLATE 65. E. J. MUYBRIDGE ("HELIOS"). SHIPPING IN SITKA HARBOR. ALASKA. 1868. F. P

PLATE 66. E. J. MUYBRIDGE. INDIAN VILLAGE, FORT WRANGLE, NEAR MOUTH OF THE STACHINE RIVER. ALASKA. 1868. F. P

PLATE 67. E. J. MUYBRIDGE. FORT TONGASS FROM ACROSS THE CHANNEL. ALASKA. 1868. F. P

PLATE 68. E. J. MUYBRIDGE ("HELIOS"). KEE-KOO-TOO-YEM (WATER ASLEEP), MIRROR LAKE, VALLEY OF THE YOSEMITE. 1867. H. UCB

PLATE 69. E. J. MUYBRIDGE ("HELIOS"). TO-COY-AE (SHADE TO INDIAN BABY BASKET), VALLEY OF THE YOSEMITE. 1867. F. UCB

PLATE 70. E. J. MUYBRIDGE. MIRROR LAKE, VALLEY OF THE YOSEMITE. NO. 25. 1872. M, MMA

PLATE 71. E. J. MUYBRIDGE. VALLEY OF THE YOSEMITE FROM MOSQUITO CAMP. NO. 22. 1872. M. UCLA

PLATE 72. E. J. MUYBRIDGE. LOYA (THE SENTINEL), VALLEY OF THE YOSEMITE. NO 14. 1872. M. UCLA

PLATE 73. E. J. MUYBRIDGE. GLACIER ROCK, VALLEY OF THE YOSEMITE. NO. 27. 1872. M. UCLA

PLATE 74. E. J. MUYBRIDGE. CATHEDRAL SPIRES,
VALLEY OF THE YOSEMITE. NO. 8. 1872.

PLATE 75. E. J. MUYBRIDGE. FALLS OF THE YOSEMITE, FROM GLACIER ROCK. NO. 36. 1872. M. UCLA

PLATE 76. E. J. MUYBRIDGE. YOSEMITE CLIFF AT THE SUMMIT OF THE FALL. NO. 45. 1872. M. UCLA

PLATE 77. E. J. MUYBRIDGE. ANCIENT GLACIER CHANNEL, LAKE TENAYA, SIERRA NEVADA MOUNTAINS. NO. 47. 1872. M. OM

PLATE 78. E. J. MUYBRIDGE. CLOUD'S REST, VALLEY OF THE YOSEMITE. NO. 40. 1872. M. UCLA

PLATE 79. E. J. MUYBRIDGE. TISAYAC (PINE MOUNTAIN), VALLEY OF THE YOSEMITE. NO. 43. 1872. M. UCLA

PLATE 80. E. J. MUYBRIDGE. TENAYA CANON FROM UNION POINT, VALLEY OF THE YOSEMITE. NO. 35. 1872. M. UCLA

PLATE 81. E. J. MUYBRIDGE. VALLEY OF THE YOSEMITE FROM GLACIER POINT. NO. 33. 1872. M. UCLA

PLATE 82. E. J. MUYBRIDGE. TUTOKANULA (THE GREAT CHIEF), "EL CAPITAN," 3500 FEET HIGH, VALLEY OF THE YOSEMITE. NO. 9. 1872. M. UCLA

PLATE 83. E. J. MUYBRIDGE. THE DOMES, FROM GLACIER ROCK, VALLEY OF THE YOSEMITE. NO. 37. 1872. M. P

1963. Quezaltenango, Crater of Volcan

Quetzeltenango, Guatemala

PLATE 84A. E. J. MUYBRIDGE. QUEZALTENANGO, CRATER OF THE THE VOLCANO, GUATEMALA. 1875. s. p

PLATE 84B. E. J. MUYBRIDGE. TRAIL TO UNION POINT (YOSEMITE). ABOUT 1872. s. imp/geh

1496—Trail to Union Point,

PLATE 85A. E. J. MUYBRIDGE. YOSEMITE STUDIES.
NO. 1447. ABOUT 1872. s. IMP/GEH

PLATE 85B. E. J. MUYBRIDGE. YOSEMITE STUDIES.
NO. 1490. ABOUT 1872. s. IMP/GEH

PLATE 86. E. J. MUYBRIDGE. PI-WI-ACK (SHOWER
OF STARS), VERNAL FALL, 400 FEET
FALL, VALLEY OF THE YOSEMITE. NO.
29. 1872. M. P

PLATE 87. E. J. MUYBRIDGE. PI-WY-ACK (SHOWER OF STARS), VERNAL FALL, 400 FEET FALL, VALLEY OF THE YOSEMITE. NO. 28. 1872. M. P

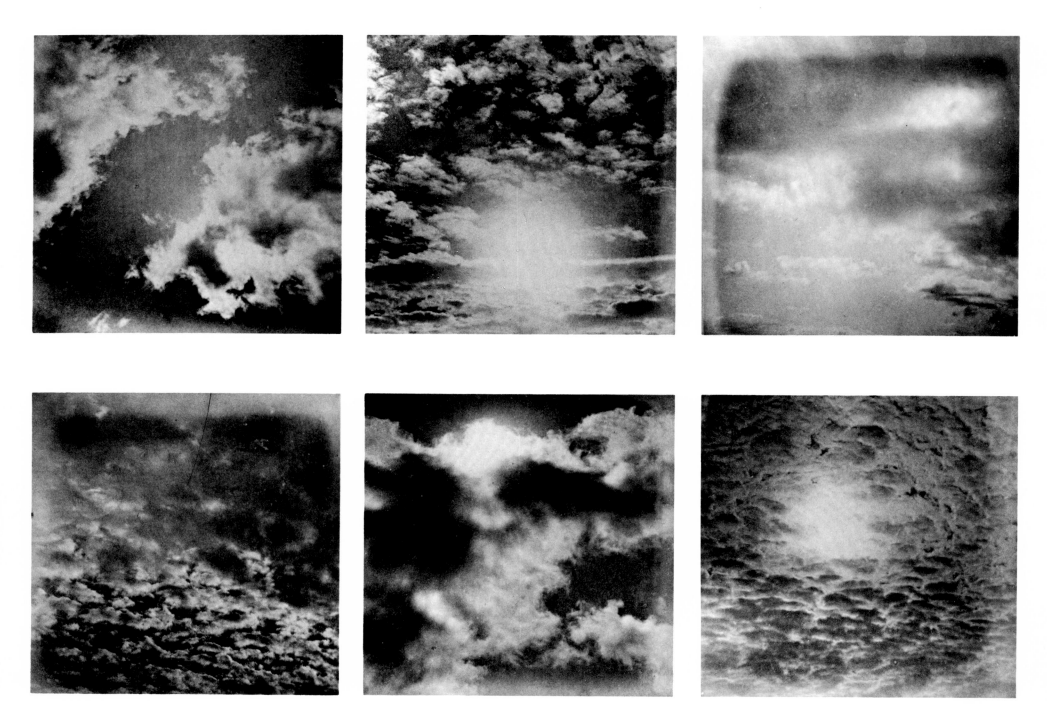

PLATE 88. E. J. MUYBRIDGE. STUDIES OF CLOUDS. NOS. 535, 536, 537, 541, 544, 548. ABOUT 1869. ½S. UCB

Andrew Joseph Russell

1830-1902

Russell, like many other image makers of the nineteenth-century American frontier, was skilled in sketching, oil painting, and wet-plate photography. From his Nunda, New York, job teaching penmanship—probably the only "artistic" avenue in the public schools of his day—Russell went to New York City and set up a studio. A career combining painting and photography was common enough, and a number of prominent artist-photographers established similar studios: the Bierstadt Brothers of New Bedford, Massachusetts (Figs. 33, 34), Solomon Carvalho on Fremont's expedition, John Wesley Jones (Figs. 38, 39), and Nahl and Wenderoth in California. Although they were all practicing painters, they took up photography as a way to augment the visual chronicle of their time.

Russell went beyond using the camera simply for making notes; he found the photograph esthetically satisfying in many of the same ways as the scene itself. He described Spectre Lake in the Uinta Mountains, Utah Territory, thus: "To say the sun reveals untold beauties, is commonplace indeed. Words cannot express or describe it. But the truthful camera tells the tale, and tells it well."[167] He compared the actual scene to the glass plate he made of it in August 1869 and noted: "The picture developed finely, and, forgetting the color in the magnificent effect, a picture, clean [and] sharp, and a peculiar softness pervading the whole, reconciled me at once to the loss of color."[168]

Russell's work includes numerous paintings—mainly landscapes and portraits—most of which are apparently lost, although in 1892 a few were with a family in Nunda. Among the missing works are a number of vast panoramas Russell painted in

give a detailed explanation and record, but few of the extant views convey any sense of the war itself.

The album in which these war photographs were gathered was regarded by its owners—the Haupt family, who kept it until 1898—as containing "war pictures." The name seems strange since there are almost no scenes of actual combat. Instead the photographs require the viewer to supply information and to know the time and place the photographs were made. In much the same way, a viewer of a stop-action, instantaneous photograph of a waterfall has to visually supply the movement of the water.

After the war Russell moved between the East and Omaha, where he was the official photographer for the Union Pacific Railroad [170] (Figs. 59, 173) and alternated photography with painting. He apparently painted portraits of a Nunda family in 1868/1869 and reported on local and major national

events in his letters from the West to the *Nunda News*.[171] A note in the Haupt album declares that "after the war Russell was many years an artist on the staff of Frank Leslie's Magazine." Leslie reproduced woodengravings after Russell's photographs, but nothing indicates that Russell was otherwise one of Leslie's graphic artists.

Russell's most important extant work describes the impact of the railways on America. "The continental iron band now unites the distant portions of the Republic and opens up to commerce, navigation, and enterprise the vast unpeopled plains."[172] The railroad images include a great many sequence shots, which would provide a record of the actual construction had they been exposed on motion-picture film. Over 200 large glass-plate railroad views, 10 by 13 inches, are in the collection of The Oakland Museum History Department.[173] They include scenes like the bridge across Dale Creek

Hornellsville (now Hornell), New York. A spectator at an 1862 exhibition of Russell's paintings observed that they were based on photographs and remarked on the "volumes of truth" in the convincing detail with which Russell portrayed dying Civil War soldiers.[169]

Russell's Civil War photographs still exist and are well represented in the National Archives, Washington, and in two collections in the Prints and Photographs Division of the Library of Congress. These photographs were made while Russell served as a captain in the U.S. Military Railroad Construction Corps under the command of Gen. A. Haupt.

In the clear, close-up photographs made during the Civil War Russell compiled a virtual list of fortifications, buildings, and equipment (Fig. 172), and there is little about this set of images that goes beyond a catalogue of objects. As a group the prints

ABOVE LEFT:

172. A. J. Russell. View of Railroad from an Elevation of 1000 Feet (with developing box). 1867/1868. s. P

173. Attributed to A. J. Russell. Roundhouse and Locomotive. 1863–1866. F. NA

(Fig. 174), an artists' camp (Fig. 175), workmen in ordinary poses (Pl. 94), and squaws gambling.

Russell said of photographing the Indians:

I set up the instrument, took the picture, made a failure as they supposed that I could take them whether they stood still or not. The second attempt was a success. . . . It made a unique group. There were no two dressed alike. . . . The squaws were dressed and painted for the pictures (also) . . . what pleased them most was that I got the papooses . . . and as they crowded around me they would shout and laugh as they recognized each others' faces. . . . They believe that when their picture is taken, that white man see what they are doing no matter where they are. . . . They were after me to-day to take picture of white man that stole a gun from one of the tribe. They said you take his picture, we catch um.[174]

Much of the material in Oakland is identified in the emulsions by numbers and titles such as "Mormon family" (Fig. 176) and "Engineer's office." Many, however, list the name of a specific subject and its

location. In all there is just one identified view of Russell's photographic wheelwagon and only one picture of Russell himself—a tiny shot of his head sticking out of a sleeping bag. But if the photographic record is sometimes sparse, details are plentiful in Russell's lively, articulate letters home.

When he joined the King Survey of the Bear River area of Utah, Russell again recorded his adventures for the Nunda press. King, Russell notes, "has been on this mission for three years and has made a complete geographical, geological and botanical survey of a great extent . . . and has ascended in the three years over three hundred mountain peaks, taken their heights . . . notes the heads and courses of their rivers. . . ." Russell adds, "I took a great many magnificent views in this vicinity which I will take pleasure in exhibiting for your inspection when I return to Nunda."[175]

A. J. Russell was mainly a photographer of trans-

174. A. J. Russell. Dale Creek Bridge from Below. 1867/1868. S. P

175. A. J. Russell. Artists at Breakfast. Uintah Mountains. 1867/1868. S. P

RIGHT:
176. A. J. Russell. Mormon Family, Great Salt Lake, Great Salt Lake Valley. 1867/1868. I. YU

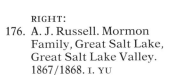

portation, and as such he was a major talent. He joined Clarence King (Fig. 177) in August 1869 and later came away in awe of the achievement of King's party, both as a survey team and, more remarkable, as a group of trained young scientists out to conquer mountains that were largely unknown.[176] King's sense of mission is expressed in his writings, which link the glory of the high art of Europe with the mountains of the West. He saw a correlation between art and the landscape of the Sierra Nevada.

King's awe of the mountains' grandeur was tempered by the restraint of his scientific discipline. His approach was impressive to Russell, whose view of landscape photography was also functional, inasmuch as he had been sent to record the mountains for railroad progress reports.

The wild landscape of the West is reflected in Russell's many wide, distant views with salient geological features highlighted. The organic forms are given definition in Skull Rock (Pl. 91) by the dramatic placement of a minute figure silhouetted against the sky. At first glance the rocks, tumbled about from the pile they originally joined, seem a playground. But the men, barely seen at a boulder in the foreground, reveal that only a colossus could have arranged the scene. On the mountains of the Green River (Pl. 99) the one man visible in the crotch of the mountain conveys the extreme loneliness of the place. At the same time, the figure belies the totally inhospitable nature of the terrain.

Isolated high country seriously limited the way photographers like Russell could record scenes; every aspect of outdoor picture taking had to be adjusted to the hardships of life with frontier parties. Russell found that even water, which was so plentiful in the "big great West," was generally too alkaline to use for developing negatives. On more than one occasion he walked some fifty miles carrying good water while he scouted for special views. Twice his horses bolted on the steep hills carrying away his prized equipment.

Clearly the ability to cope with the challenge of

hardship attracted men like Russell because they could invent solutions to the problems of wilderness. Russell reported in *The Philadelphia Photographer* that he had designed a new camera box for the mammoth-plate machine. His invention, he explained, would make a 17-by-21-inch plate camera lighter than an ordinary 10-by-12-inch one. Russell claimed, too, that the new design would make picture taking more convenient and prove more durable than the earlier apparatus.

The early photographic efforts to capture the images of western landscape did much to heighten the public awareness of the natural monuments and the need to conserve those areas. As only a few hardy travelers knew the Sierra Nevada and Yellowstone, the work of photographers and painters gave crucial evidence of the need to protect them from future abuse. The first national parks owed their existence to the visual record made on the early surveys and explorations.

In 1869 the Union Pacific published an album of fifty albumen prints of Russell's views, but neither these nor the far larger group of 452 stereographic glass-plate negatives brought him fame.[177] Ironically, his most famous photograph—of the joining of the rails at Promontory, Utah—was long thought to be by another photographer; the illustration in *Harper's Weekly*, 5 June 1869, credited "Savage," and the confusion persisted in most printed sources. In the Promontory scene, as in many of the larger panoramic photographs, Russell's composition is similar to the grand views popular with the landscape painters of the West, like Thomas Hill (Fig. 87) and Keith. As Russell himself was an experienced painter, his unfailing eye framed wide-scale "views" that established him with the best of his contemporaries in photography.

After the Promontory views Russell recorded at least forty large glass plates on a trip to Sacramento.[178] Afterward he returned to New York, where he established a studio at 360 Bowery and produced photographs for weeklies such as *Leslie's Illustrated Weekly Magazine*.[179]

177. A. J. Russell. Surveying Under Difficulties. 1869.
I. YU

PLATE 89. A. J. RUSSELL. MALLOY'S CUT, NEAR SHERMAN (WYOMING). 1867/1868. I. YU

PLATE 90. A. J. RUSSELL. HANGING ROCK, FOOT OF ECHO CANON (UTAH). 1867/1868. I. YU

PLATE 91. A. J. RUSSELL. SKULL ROCK, DALE CREEK CANON (WYOMING). 1867/1868. I. YU

PLATE 92. A. J. RUSSELL. GRANITE CANON, FROM THE WATER TANK (WYOMING). 1867/1868. I YU

PLATE 93. A. J. RUSSELL. COAL BED OF BEAR RIVER (UTAH). 1867/1868. I. YU

PLATE 94. A. J. RUSSELL. BUILDING TUNNEL NO. 3, NEAR WEBER CANON (UTAH). 1867/1868. I. YU

PLATE 95. A. J. RUSSELL. TEMPORARY AND PERMANENT BRIDGES & CITADEL ROCK, GREEN RIVER (WYOMING). 1867/1868. I. YU

PLATE 96. A. J. RUSSELL. WEBER VALLEY, FROM WILHELMINA PASS (UTAH). 1867/1868. I. YU

PLATE 97. A. J. RUSSELL. MONUMENT ROCK, MOUTH
OF ECHO CANON (UTAH). 1867/1868. I YU

PLATE 98. A. J. RUSSELL. HIGH BLUFF, BLACK BUTTES (WYOMING). 1867/1868. I. YU

PLATE 99. A. J. RUSSELL. ON MOUNTAINS OF GREEN RIVER, SMITH BUTTE IN FOREGROUND (WYOMING). 1867/1868. I. YU

PLATE 100. A. J. RUSSELL. CASTLE ROCKS, GREEN RIVER VALLEY (UTAH?). 1867/1868. I. YU

PLATE 101. A. J. RUSSELL. RIPPLE LAKE, WHITE PINE CANON (NEVADA?). 1867/1868. I. YU

PLATE 102. A. J. RUSSELL. SILVER MINING DISTRICT, DALE CREEK (WYOMING). 1867/1868. I. YU

William Henry Jackson

1843-1942

As a young man Jackson was an enthusiastic diarist who later became an avid correspondent and self-publicist; as a result, his life and work are better known than those of his contemporaries. Jackson's photographs are also preserved in greater numbers than those of many others, since he was in commercial photography for all but the eight years he spent with the F. V. Hayden Survey. The photographs themselves are, of course, the most important evidence of a camera artist's career.

During the time he worked for Hayden—between 1870 and 1878—Jackson evolved from a novice to a journeyman photographer. As a youth he had been a retoucher of portraits in various New England galleries, including C. C. Schoonmaker's of Troy, New York, and the Vermont studios of Frank Mowry in Rutland and F. Styles of Burlington. But a retoucher would not ordinarily be involved in the photographic aspect of a portrait studio,[180] and it is not surprising that when Jackson went West in 1866 as an ox-team driver in a train of freight wagons, he made no photographs of record. There is no evidence that he was even skilled as a photographer. He did have a strong visual orientation, however, and sketched profusely. To judge from the drawings, Jackson did not have an intense consciousness of the landscape but was much more interested in camp life and the characters of the trail. His sketches do not suggest the work of a person familiar with sketching quickly outdoors. (Fig. 178), nor do they have the vivacity and realistic quality of the contemporary woodengravings in *Harper's Weekly* and *Leslie's Illustrated Weekly Magazine*.[181]

Jackson was aware that he was participating in

178. W. H. Jackson. Untitled. Near Nebraska City, June 1866. Ink on paper. NPS

an epoch pregnant with history worth recording. On his first journey West he was much better at words than pictures and wrote long letters home in a flowing, descriptive prose in which events and personalities assume a presence they lack in his drawings. Abandoning for the moment the directions his talents as an artist and writer might have taken him, he and his younger brother plunged into the business of photography in Omaha, the headquarters for the Union Pacific Railroad. The Jacksons' enterprise was financed by their parents, with William assuming the responsibility for the outdoor work and Ed operating the portrait studio.[182]

Jackson Brothers, during the first year of operation in 1867, made photographs typical of most studios in the United States at that time. Jackson recollected much later that the clientele included "straight portrait jobs; group pictures of lodges, church societies and political clubs; and outdoor

179. W. H. Jackson. Unidentified (Utah ?). 1869. s. MMA

shots that gratified civic pride. There were many commissions to photograph shop fronts, and, occasionally, interiors. Now and then, too, somebody would order pictures of his new house; or of his big barn, and along with it the livestock."[183]

Jackson realized from the outset that he was an outdoor photographer, and his photographs of Indian tribes around Omaha of 1868 were a bold step away from the conventional portrait photographer's fare.

During the summer of 1869 he made his first extensive campaign of photography away from the conveniences of Omaha. With A. C. Hull he embarked along the route of the Union Pacific barely a month after the golden spike had been driven at Promontory, Utah. Jackson's diary for the summer reveals a great deal about the daily life of an outdoor photographer and is one of the few extant records of a photographer's initial experience working under "expeditionary" circumstances. Jackson was relatively inexperienced at landscape work, and his journal reveals the process of self-education by trial and error that was then commonplace, if not necessary, among outdoor photographers.

He left Omaha with Hull on 22 June 1869 with equipment for printing and finishing the photographs as well as the facilities for making negatives. The two men planned to meet running expenses by selling photographs along the way, which necessitated more gear than was convenient for travel. The equipment—glass, cameras, and chemicals—was contained in a box fifteen by fifteen by thirty inches that was convertible to a dark chamber. Jackson recounted that the box was no problem when they were directly on the line of the railroad but became a substantial burden away from it. Jackson and Hull were by no means as experienced at working away from civilization as Watkins, O'Sullivan, and Savage were. The very nature of Jackson's equipment kept him near the tracks, and the manner in which he and Hull financed their trip dictated that towns be their main subjects. The

resulting photographs differ little from those made earlier around Omaha.

Jackson's journal is very informative about the pair's manner of hustling customers. They would arrive at a town like Cheyenne, Wyoming, or Corinne, Utah, and probe the streets photographing stores, banks, other prosperous businesses, as well as the houses of the wealthiest residents, then would attempt to sell the owner or proprietor the photograph by confronting him with the finished print. Booming railroad towns (Fig. 179) brought prosperity to many enterprises, and the photographers overlooked no potential customer. Jackson recounted his pitch to Madame Cleveland, the keeper of Cheyenne's most prosperous brothel, who was plied with two bottles of wine until she was "hot and heavy for some large pictures to frame.[184] Jackson described photographing Madame Cleveland with her girls on a Saturday afternoon, making three negatives of which only one was successful. That evening he retouched the minute spots on the week's negatives and varnished them. Sunday morning he arose at seven when he first sensitized the printing paper, then proceeded to make twelve good prints by two in the afternoon, and at five he had twenty photographs printed, toned, dried, and mounted ready for delivery the next day. The pattern of making negatives during the weekdays and retouching and printing them by working Saturday night and all day Sunday continued for the rest of the trip. The sale of photographs to Madame Cleveland and others grossed Jackson and Hull sixty dollars in pocket the day they departed by train for Corinne.

Jackson had two cameras—one for stereoscopic and one for eight- by- ten-inch negatives. The working procedure called for Hull to act as the salesman and canvasser, drumming up business while Jackson worked in the darkroom coating and sensitizing the plates as well as choosing the camera angles.

As they got farther west, the towns were smaller and prosperous clients harder to find, and in Uinta, Utah, for example, they sustained themselves by

180. W. H. Jackson. Dale Creek Bridge. No. 198. 1869.
S. MMA

selling photographs to the railroad workers. Their customers were not only the engineers and trainmen, who wanted portraits with their locomotives, but also the laborers, who were photographed in groups as they worked on tunnels, bridges (Fig. 180), and rock cuts (Pl. 103).

Jackson and Hull were not deeply committed to any set of subjects and photographed what their customers needed. Indeed, their longest stint of work outdoors on subjects of pure landscape, in Weber and Echo canyons, came as the result of a request by the railroad porter in Cheyenne, who had placed an order for a thousand views—presumably to sell to passengers. During three months in the field Jackson spent about one month, beginning 13 August 1869, photographing landscape features such as Skull Rock, Castle Rock, and the Great Eastern as well as the Echo and Weber canyons. He reported one of these sessions in a journal, saying that he made three or four negatives with

"Ben and the Keeper of the Hash House as accessory ornaments (Fig. 181)."[185] At this point Jackson was by no means primarily a landscape photographer; he was a journalist working with a camera, seeking the subjects the public wanted recorded. There is scant evidence that he had any more than a passing interest in pure landscape in 1869. He catalogued only forty-five landscape negatives from the excursion along the railroad route.[186]

Jackson's diaries reveal the process by which he became aware of landscape. On the train from Cheyenne to Corinne, before ever seeing the canyons he was to photograph, he observed that "the scenery of Echo and Weber *appeared* magnificent and *will* keep me continually perplexed."[187] Jackson revised the statement in later versions of his autobiography, putting it in the past tense to erase the suggestion that he arrived at the canyon lands with any preconceived idea. Photographs he had seen of the places he would soon visit suggested the challenge nature would pose for him. Jackson's diary also records that he knew A. J. Russell and C. R. Savage by reputation before actually meeting them. Savage, of Salt Lake City, sold him photographic materials—at a considerable profit. Jackson became friendly with Russell's printer in Echo and studied the negatives of his very accomplished competitor, whom he met a month later.[188] Jackson must have been very impressed with Russell's work, for some of his own photographs around Echo Canyon (Fig. 64) are pastiches of Russell's images. Jackson marked his negatives from Echo and Weber canyons with the monogram W H J in a stylized circle to indelibly sign his work; the mark does not appear on any other negatives from that time (Pl. 109).

In 1869 Jackson made enough photographs along the route of the Union Pacific to impress F. V. Hayden that he was competent in landscape work. Actually, until Jackson spent the season of 1870 in the field as a volunteer with Hayden's U.S. Geological and Geographical Survey of the Territories, he had not made a very significant body of outdoor work. Jackson's photographs from the 1869 Union

Pacific excursion were donated to the survey after he became a salaried employee in 1871, and these, along with his production of 1870–1875 were carefully listed and described in printed booklets. These are extremely useful documents for charting Jackson's first years as a landscape photographer.

Before 1870 Jackson had not established an esthetic direction for himself. He knew portrait work was unsuitable and cast about for viable ways to make a living outdoors; he later recounted that the Hayden Expedition was "priceless, it gave me a career."[189] Hayden led the expedition during 1870 to the Black Hills of Wyoming, the North Platte and Sweetwater rivers, South Pass and the Mau-

181. W. H. Jackson. Pulpit Rock, Echo, Utah. 1869. F. ANS

182. W. H. Jackson. Hot Springs, on Gardiner's River,
Upper Basins (Thomas Moran standing). 1871.
s. MMA

vaises Terres, Fort Bridger, into the Uinta Mountains, down the Green River, through Bridger's Pass to Fort Sanders, and from there along the foothill ranges to Pike's Peak. Like a child thrown into a pool, Jackson learned to swim as a landscape photographer by suddenly encountering inaccessible terrain he might never have approached otherwise. Between 1870 and 1873 only a handful of his negatives were devoted to ethnology each season; the vast majority were photographs of pure landscape.

Like Clarence King, F. V. Hayden was a geologist with respect for the role of the artist and his usefulness to the ends of a scientific survey. King, Hayden's rival, shared John Ruskin's love of beauty in the sublime details of nature, subjects the camera was uniquely capable of recording and that were the focus of the geologist's attention during the normal course of his work. Hayden, on the other hand, was influenced by the monumental work of such artists as S. R. Gifford (Fig. 92) and Thomas Moran, who each accompanied him—Gifford in 1870 and Moran in 1871. Their place on a geological expedition was appropriate since they both saw geology as one of the building blocks in the macrostructure of panoramic landscape painting. Jackson spent a great deal of his time with Gifford and Moran (Fig. 182) and from them learned to prize the integrated panorama over isolated details of landscape as the most important element of a picture.

Jackson's work of 1869, before the Hayden Survey, already showed the seeds of an interest in geological subjects. The rock formations he photographed, however, were chosen for their beauty (Fig. 183) and were not of complex enough structure to interest the working geologist. Jackson soon learned that subjects of use to geologists were indeed subtler visually than his early rock studies but were not lacking in their own grandeur (Pl. 104); at times the survey photographs were virtually empty of overt subject (Fig. 184). Unlike the Rocky Mountain panoramas, these photographs

were made as tools for the geologists, yet they also express Jackson's affinity for the enigmatic forms in nature that reappears in his Yellowstone photographs.

If in 1870 Jackson was challenged by motifs of such delicate beauty and visual mystery that they resisted easy treatment, his task in 1871 and 1872 was the opposite. The photographs from the season of 1871 in the Great Hot Springs on Gardiner's

River, the Great Falls, and the Grand Canyon of the Yellowstone, and from a return trip to the same regions in 1872, yielded subjects of compelling visual interest that the photographer was required to isolate rather than treat as elements in a broad pictorial matrix. The approach was a complete about-face from that of the previous season, when Jackson's most successful photographs were taken from mountain peaks; he was now in the valleys focusing on specific subjects, and he did not fully succeed in altering his point of view.

RIGHT:
183. W. H. Jackson. Tower on Castle Rock. No. 1112.
Published by Jackson Bros. 1869. s. P

The 1871 season proved to be a study session in preparation for the following year. Jackson appears to have been overwhelmed by the unearthly subjects he first confronted in the Geyser Basin along the Fire Hole River, for his photographs of these sites are general overviews, lacking clarity or conviction about the subjects themselves. The following year he probed the form and structure of that "moonscape" (Pl. 116), establishing the classic points of view that most perfectly described the basins, grottoes, and geysers. The Mammoth Spring, with its concentric tiers, is blandly treated in the first attempt but in the second (Fig. 185) becomes a powerful compositional element, especially in the eleven-by-fourteen-inch photographs he began to take in 1872. In 1875 he was to return to the Geyser Basin with a camera capable of receiving twenty-by-twenty-four-inch glass plates; the resulting work would prove to be the synthesis of his two earlier campaigns (Pl. 115).

Jackson apparently did not accept the limitations of the camera technology of the seventies. At Geyser Basin in 1871 he pressed his equipment to record the steam billowing from the mud and the jets of hot water rising from the rock fissures, but his cameras were incapable of reproducing such subtle atmospheric effects, and he was forced to retouch his negatives to add the necessary steam and rising water. The negatives must have been unconvincing, for they received very little circulation, and indeed, their relative failure might have prompted Jackson's return to Yellowstone in 1872. On the second trip he devoted his time to stationary subjects like the Mammoth Spring, which were dramatic in themselves but were effectively photographed with the available materials. Jackson came away from the second visit with unmanipulated negatives of all Yellowstone's major features. These photographs were widely circulated in the form of bound albums that were instrumental in bringing the glory of Yellowstone to the attention of senators and congressmen, who declared it a national park the same year.[190]

184. W. H. Jackson. Bad Lands on Black's Fork. Wyoming. 1870.
H. ANS

185. W. H. Jackson. Mammoth Hot Springs. Gardiner's River. 1871.
I. ANS

186. W. H. Jackson. Cave Town on the Rio de Chelley. No. 282. 1875. H. ANS

During the seasons of 1873 and 1874 Jackson's talent as a landscape photographer crested; 1873 was his first season outside Yellowstone without the presence of a painter as a guiding influence. He had certainly benefited from his association with Gifford and Moran. However, photography could still not match some of the motifs open to artists —color and motion in particular. The painter could set good examples for seeing the structure, order, and composition of nature, but the painted models became a hindrance if the photographer followed them too literally. Jackson was artistically on his own between 1873 and 1875, a time when the goals and structure of the Hayden Survey were themselves changing. During these years he traveled in a small party over great distances to photograph

exactly what he felt was worthy, and this independence is evident in the photographs. It is perhaps coincidental that Jackson was under the immediate supervision of J. T. Gardner, a topographer, who had already had experience with Watkins in Yosemite and O'Sullivan in Nevada when he worked with the Whitney Survey and the King Survey, which had just come to its official end.

1873 was an important year because Jackson and his party ranged across the entire east front of the Rocky Mountains from New Mexico to Wyoming— landscape that Jackson photographed intensively on eleven-by-fourteen-inch plates. An accident caused his pack mule, Gimlet, to fall, and most of the plates were broken. Luckily, the Mountain of the Holy Cross was photographed after the accident, and the results remain some of the most memorable of Jackson's work. Jackson was the first to photograph the Holy Cross,[191] and while these are not his strongest images, they have had the longest life, a longevity due in part to the fame and popularity of Thomas Moran's painting of the same subject, based on one of Jackson's photographs.

The Mountain of the Holy Cross (Pl. 119) is but one instance of an underlying romantic sensibility in Jackson's photographs. Consciously or not, he had absorbed the esthetic of picturesque romanticism. The inherent drama of a panorama extending miles into the distance was his preference, and wherever possible a figure was tastefully introduced in a manner far more successful that the rigidly posed figures of the 1869 series or the overly casual figures that appear, sometimes as if by accident, in the photographs of the 1870 series.

Jackson's work of 1874 and 1875 represents his maturity as a landscape photographer (Pl. 110). The photographs have a self-conscious artfulness that is as evident as naïveté was in the 1869 series. The later photographs are characterized by a gentle and harmonious transition from foreground to middle ground to remote distance. The foreground is often dominated by a rock or tree; the middle ground frequently contains a sinuous river or valley running obliquely into the distance as a counterpoint to the horizon. In 1874/1875 Jackson had the structural aspects of landscape at his command, and the photographs reveal a consistent sense of design. The artfulness is enhanced by Jackson's new capacity to render a cloud-filled sky with a success equal to that of Muybridge's Yosemite views.

The degree to which Jackson had become purely a landscape photographer is evident in his treatment of the remains of lost Indian civilizations, which played a prominent role in his work of 1874 and 1875. Jackson's reminiscences suggest how excited he was about these subjects. However, the excitement is absent from the photographs. He photographed the ruins at Mancos Canyon and Canyon de Chelly (Fig. 186) with the perception of the documentarian; he did not attempt to make pictures of the ruins but rather created archeological records.

Timothy O'Sullivan had preceded Jackson to Canyon de Chelly in 1873, and a comparison of their work there reveals the esthetic distance between them (Pl. 62). Jackson photographed the ruins from a distance in several exposures, made several exposures of the ruins at the bottom, and made several more inside the cliff dwellings. None of these is as carefully designed as O'Sullivan's Ancient Ruins in the Canyon de Chelly, which evokes the mystery and drama of the place. Jackson had no less wonder at the ruins but expressed it far more literally.

Jackson became deeply involved with living Indian tribes as well and made many photographs of the Moquis pueblos in 1875 (Fig. 187). These lack the careful design of his panoramic landscapes of the previous season but are more compassionate human documents. The momentum Jackson developed through his activity with lost civilizations and living tribes carried him through 1876, the centennial year, for which he built models of the pueblos. These were exhibited at the Philadelphia Exposition, and Jackson spent the season as master of ceremonies at the display, answering questions from the public.

At the very time his talent as a landscape photographer reached its zenith Jackson's energies were temporarily diverted to ethnography; he made many Indian portraits and another series of archeological sites. He was to begin active landscape work again in 1879 but under different circumstances and in search of new effects.

Always ambitious, Jackson admitted in his autobiography that he was dissatisfied with his salary, which he compared to a government clerk's. When the Hayden Survey ended in 1879 with the creation of the United States Geological Survey, he set out on his own.[192] Jackson bought the equipment he had used while with Hayden and established the Jackson Photographic Company in a newly built studio in Denver.

187. W. H. Jackson. View from Tequa Towards Moqui. No. 296. 1875. H. ANS

The years with the Hayden Survey allowed Jackson to pursue the landscape photographer's equivalent of art for art's sake in recording remote sites that no one might visit again for decades. In 1874 and 1875 particularly, Jackson had photographed only what pleased him. His new business, like any other commercial venture, depended on the public demand, and Jackson necessarily photographed what other people wanted to see—and to buy. This restriction took him again along the railroad routes, and one of his best customers was the Denver and Rio Grande Railway, from which he received a large commission in 1881. Subsequently he became well known as a photographer to many other railroads, a position for which his survey work was the perfect preparation. Of the Hayden Survey years Jackson said, "If any work that I have done should have value beyond my own lifetime, I believe it will be the happy labors of the decade 1869–1879."[193]

Jackson's photographs of the 1880s and later assumed a character quite different from that of his survey work. He often carried a mammoth-plate camera slightly smaller than the one for twenty-by-twenty-four-inch plates he had used with limited success on the 1875 Hayden Survey. His landscapes of the eighties are artistically dependent on the precedents Watkins and Muybridge set in the sixties and seventies; Jackson perfected Muybridge's technique of posing a figure in landscape to indicate scale and create a picturesque effect (Pl. 126). He had included figures in many of his survey landscapes but never in order to achieve the narrative quality of his later work.

Through the wide distribution of the photographs he made for the western railroads—and through later work made into postcards by the Detroit Publishing Company—Jackson influenced the public awareness of landscape perhaps more than any other photographer of his generation. Watkins attempted throughout his career to establish a commercial clientele similar to Jackson's—but without the success of his younger colleague.

226

PLATE 103. W. H. JACKSON. BURNING ROCK CUT, NEAR GREEN RIVER STATION, WYOMING TERRITORY, 1869. H. ANS

PLATE 104. W. H. JACKSON. UINTAH MOUNTAINS FROM PHOTOGRAPH RIDGE (UTAH). 1870. H. ANS

PLATE 105. W. H. JACKSON. ROCKS BELOW PLATTE CANON (COLORADO). 1870. H. ANS

87. VIEW ON THE SWEETWATER,

PLATE 106. W. H. JACKSON. VIEW ON THE SWEETWATER (WYOMING). 1870. H. ANS

PLATE 107. W. H. JACKSON. STUDY ALONG THE SUMMIT OF THE GRANITE RIDGE (WYOMING). 1870. H. ANS

PLATE 108A. W. H. JACKSON. BALANCED ROCKS ON CROW CREEK, NEAR SHERMAN (WYOMING). 1869. s. p

PLATE 108B. W. H. JACKSON. THE ELK, CERFUS CANADENSIS. 1871. s. p

PLATE 109. W. H. JACKSON. TEAPOT ROCK, NEAR GREEN RIVER STATION (WYOMING). 1869. F. ANS

248. UNCOMPAGRE.

PLATE 110. W. H. JACKSON. UNCOMPAGRE (PEAK, COLORADO). 1875. H. ANS

PLATE 111. W. H. JACKSON. BEAVER'S WORK. 1870. H. ANS

COLUMNAR BASALTS ON YELLOWSTONE RIVER

PLATE 112. W. H. JACKSON. COLUMNAR BASALTS ON THE YELLOWSTONE (WYOMING). 1873. I. ANS

PLATE 113. W. H. JACKSON. SHOSHONE FALLS, LOOKING DOWN THE CANON (IDAHO). NO. 1112. AFTER 1880. M. LL

204. MUD GEYSER IN ACTION.

PLATE 115.
W. H. JACKSON. MAMMOTH
HOT SPRINGS ON
GARDINER'S RIVER
(WYOMING). NO. 1091.
AFTER 1880.
M. MMA

PLATE 114. W. H. JACKSON. MUD GEYSER IN ACTION, THE GREAT HOT SPRINGS ON GARDINER'S RIVER (WYOMING). 1871.
F. ANS

1091 MAMMOTH HOT SPRINGS. PULPIT TERRACES.   W.H. JACKSON & C? DENVER COL.

PLATE 116. W. H. JACKSON. CRATER OF THE BEEHIVE GEYSER, THE GREAT HOT SPRINGS ON GARDINER'S RIVER (WYOMING). 1872. F. ANS

BOILING SULPHER SPRING. 266.

PLATE 117. W. H. JACKSON. BOILING SPRING AT SULPHUR MOUNTAIN (WYOMING). ABOUT 1875. F. P

PLATE 118. W. H. JACKSON. ROCHES MOUTONNEES, NEAR THE MOUNTAIN OF THE HOLY CROSS (COLORADO). 1873. I. ANS

106. MOUNTAIN OF THE HOLY-CROSS

PLATE 119. W. H. JACKSON. MOUNTAIN OF THE HOLY CROSS (COLORADO). 1873. i. ans

PLATE 120. W. H. JACKSON. TOWER OF BABEL,
GARDEN OF THE GODS (COLORADO). NO.
1007. AFTER 1880. M. P

PLATE 121. W. H. JACKSON. DIAMOND RIVER CANON
(COLORADO). NO. 1070. AFTER 1880. M. MOMA

PLATE 122. W. H. JACKSON. GATEWAY GARDEN OF THE GODS AND PIKE'S PEAK (COLORADO). NO. 1031. AFTER 1880. M. SW

1005. BALANCED ROCK. GARDEN OF THE GODS.

W.H. JACKSON & C° PHOT. DENVER.

PLATE 123. W. H. JACKSON. BALANCED ROCK, GARDEN OF THE GODS (COLORADO). NO. 1005. AFTER 1880. M. SW

PLATE 124. W. H. JACKSON. CANON OF THE RIO LAS ANIMAS (COLORADO). NO. 1077. AFTER 1880. M. DW

PLATE 125. W. H. JACKSON. THE UPPER TWIN LAKE (COLORADO). NO. 1012. AFTER 1880. M. P

PLATE 126. W. H. JACKSON. GRAND CANON OF THE
COLORADO. NO. 1069. AFTER 1880. M. LW

Notes

1. Hans Huth, *Nature and the American: Three Centuries of Changing Attitudes*, Berkeley, 1957, is the most accessible introduction to the history of nature consciousness in America.

2. Robert Taft, *Photography and the American Scene*, New York, 1938, is the best history of photography in America. The author is indebted to Taft beyond the specific citations in these notes.

3. William H. Goetzmann, *Exploration and Empire*, New York, 1966, and Richard A. Bartlett, *Great Surveys of the American West*, Norman, Oklahoma, 1962, describe the relevance of photography to the mission of the great surveys. Taft, 1938, says, "The work of the professional photographers in the West marks the beginning of a 'landscape school' in American photography, although so formal a phrase may be scarcely justified." (p. 311).

4. Coleman Sellers, "An Old Photographic Club," *Anthony's Photographic Bulletin*, 26 May-10 November 1888; "The Work of Two Amateurs," *The Philadelphia Photographer*, October 1863; see also photograph mounted in *The Philadelphia Photographer*, June 1844; Robert Culp Darrah, *Stereo Views: A History of Stereographs in America and their Collection*, Gettysburg, 1964, p. 205.

5. Richard Rudisill, *Mirror Image*, Albuquerque, 1971, chap. 5, "The 'Universal Man' and the Westering Adventurer," pp. 119-150. Figs. 12-14 reproduce landscape daguerreotypes by Samuel Bemis in the collection of IMP/GEH and dated to the early 1840s. Pp. 293-311 reproduce daguerreotypes chronicling daily life.

6. Darrah (pp. 27–34) describes the origins of the Langenheim organization and the significance of the stereograph in American culture of the nineteenth century.

7. Letter, Manuscript Division, NYPL.

8. *The Crayon*, 11 April 1855, quoted in David C. Huntington, *The Landscapes of Frederic Edwin Church: Vision of an American Era*, New York, 1966, p. 72.

9. T. F. Hardwich, *A Manual of Photographic Chemistry, including the Practice of the Collodion Process*, New York, 1858, is among the earliest American manuals on the collodion process. It was published by H. H. Snelling, who was editor of the *Photographic and Fine Art Journal*, which pioneered in the use of original photographs as illustrations (Fig. 14).

10. Gertrude Himmelfarb, *Darwin and the Darwinian Revolution*, Garden City, New York, 1962, chap. IV.

11. David Starr Jordan and Jessie Knight Jordan, "Louis Agassiz, 1807-1873," *Dictionary of American Biography*, New York, 1928, I, pp. 114-122.

12. Ibid., p. 120. Emerson's writings, particularly his small book *Nature* (Boston, 1836), were very effective in promoting landscape consciousness. See frontispiece.

13. Elizabeth Lindquist-Cock, Frederic Church's "Stereographic Vision," *Art in America* 61, no. 5 (1973), pp. 70-75; Elizabeth M. Cock, "*The Influence of Photography on American Landscape Painting*, 1839-1880," Unpublished Ph.D. dissertation, New York University, Institute of Fine Arts, 1967.

14. Julius F. Sachse, "Philadelphia's Share in the Development of Photography," *Journal of the Franklin Institute*, April 1893, pp. 284-286.

15. Sir David Brewster, *The Stereoscope: Its History, Theory and Construction*, London, 1856.

16. Darrah, fig. 1, dated "Febr. 55."

17. Taft, 1938, p. 98. The daguerreotype apparently did not surivive and was perhaps destroyed in the Boston fire of 1871.

18. I. N. Phelps Stokes, *The Hawes-Stokes Collection of American Daguerreotypes by Albert S. Southworth and Josiah Johnson Hawes*, New York, 1939, dates the daguerreotype 1845, which, on the basis of style, seems early. In his retirement Southworth was so excited by O'Sullivan's photographs of Nevada that he wrote Wheeler asking that they be exhibited at the Centennial Exposition of 1876 in Philadelphia. Letter, Wheeler Survey Records, Western Americana Collection, YU

19. Roger Fenton, *Conway in the Stereoscope*, London, 1860, illustrated with twenty stereographs exhibited at the Royal Photographic Society, 1858/1859.

20. Helmut Gernsheim and Alison Gernsheim, *The History of Photography*, London, 1969, p. 290.

21. Francis Frith, *Egypt and Palestine Photographed and Described*, London, n.d. (photographs dated 1857); The "*Queen's Bible*," Edinburgh, 1862, 2 vols., red morocco with ornamental brass, was illustrated with Frith's photographs made in Sinai 1860/1861.

22. Darrah, p. 101, quotes in full London *Times*, 1 January 1858.

23. Bourne and Shepherd, *A Permanent Record of India*, Calcutta, n.d. In print in 1973 was a catalogue listing photographs "from 1840 to the present day," most of them glass plates.

24. M. A. Root, *The Camera and Pencil; or the Heliographic Art*, Philadelphia and New York, 1864, relates Anthony's role in the survey; Taft, 1938, p. 52; Rudisill, pp. 99-101.

25. Taft, 1938, lists the following expeditionary daguerreotypes now lost: John Plumbe, 1848-1850; J. Wesley Jones, 1851; S. S. McIntyre, 1851; S. N. Carvalho, 1853; Robert Vance, 1851; J. M. Stanley, 1853; Lt. J. C. Ives, 1857; C. C. Mills, 1859; J. D. Hutton, 1859.

26. R. Bruce Duncan kindly drew my attention to the work of Mayhew and put his notes for a projected article at my disposal.

27. Howard E. Bendix, "The Stereographs of Albert Bierstadt," *Photographica* (September, October, November 1974), reproduces and describes the circumstances of the Lander Expedition. Gordon Hendricks, "The First Three Western Journeys of Albert Bierstadt," *Art Bulletin* 46 (September 1964) pp. 333-365, touches on Bierstadt's photographs.

28. Hendricks quotes in full Bierstadt's letter to *The Crayon*, 10 July 1859. Root suggests that an American school of *"Landscape Photography*, executed by artists possessing the genius of a Cole, a Durand, a Hart, a Church, a Webber, a Sontag, a Hamilton, or a Russell Smith, has hitherto received but little attention." (p. 387). Bierstadt's role as a photographer is dismissed by Elizabeth Lindquist-Cock ("Stereoscopic Photography and the Western Paintings of Albert Bierstadt," *The Art Quarterly* 33 [1970], pp. 360-378), although she reproduces paintings made under the influence of Watkins and Muybridge.

29. Robert Weinstein et al., "In San Francisco and the Mines, 1851-1856." *The American West* 4 (August 1967), pp. 40-49 and Therese Thau Heyman, *Mirror of California: Daguerreotypes*, exhibition catalogue, The Oakland Museum, 6 November 1973-27 January 1974, reproduce some of the more significant of these images. G. R. Fardon's *San Francisco Album. Photographs of the Most Beautiful and Public Buildings of San Francisco*, about 1856, is one of the earliest published collections of American outdoor photographs.

30. John Ross Dix, *Amusing and Thrilling Adventures of a California Artist While Daguerreotyping a Continent*, Boston, 1854, relates and reproduces clippings about Jones's enterprise.

31. "Jones' Pantoscope of California," *California Historical Society Quarterly* 6 (1927) p. 109 ff.

32. Mary V. Hood, "Charles L. Weed, Yosemite's First Photographer," *Yosemite Nature Notes* 38 (1959), no. 6.

33. I am grateful to Bill and Mary Hood for generously supplying information from their notes on early collodion photography in California and to Robert Weinstein for his advice on commerce in California photographs.

34. B. P. Avery, "Art Beginnings on the Pacific," *The Overland Monthly* I (July 1868), p. 34; (August 1868), p. 113.

35. Ibid., pp. 113-119.

36. E. and H. T. Anthony, *New Catalogue of Stereoscopes and Views* . . ., New York, n.d. (about 1865), and W. Langenheim, *Catalogue of Langenheim's Stereoscopic Pictures on Glass and Paper* . . ., Philadelphia, 1861, set the model for Thomas Houseworth and Co.'s *Catalogue of Photographic Views of Scenery on the Pacific Coast and Views in China and Japan*, 5th ed., San Francisco, 1869. Useful information is also in Lorraine Dexter, "Stereoscopic Photography in California," Typescript, South Woodstock, New York, n.d.

37. Houseworth, 1869, p. iv.

38. A collection of Weed's mammoth-plate photographs is in the Rare Book Room, NYPL.

39. Reduced versions of many of the NYPL prints signed by Weed are mounted in Cone and Relyea, *Sun Pictures in Yosemite*, Chicago, 1874; some of the photographs can be attributed to Muybridge. Related is *Pacific Coast Scenery*, published by Thomas Houseworth and Co., and illustrated with over one hundred stereo halves from negatives attributed to Weed and Muybridge, UCLA.

40. Charles B. Turrill, "An Early California Photographer, C. E. Watkins," *News Notes of California Libraries* 13, no. 1 (January 1918), p. 33. Diana Edkins generously supplied me with her photocopy of this scarce article.

41. "Views in Yosemite Valley," *The Philadelphia Photographer* (April 1866) p. 106.

42. Fitz Hugh Ludlow, *The Heart of the Continent*, New York, 1870, p. 412.

43. Houseworth, 1869, p. iv.

44. Ibid.

45. Watkins's advertising card, UCB; also imprinted on the verso of his stereoscopic mounts 1866-1874.

46. Mary V. Jessup Hood and Robert Bartlett Haas, "Eadweard Muybridge's Yosemite Valley Photographs, 1867-1872," *California Historical Society Quarterly* 52, no. 1 (March 1963), p. 13.

47. Examples of W. H. Jackson's mammoth plates made in Yosemite about 1889 are in the collection of the IMP/GEH.

48. Taft, 1938, pp. 277-281, relates the transition from war to railroads as subjects for photographers.

49. Henry T. Williams, *Williams' Illustrated Trans-Continental Guide* . . ., New York, 1876, p. 8.

50. Taft, 1938, p. 278, quoting the Omaha *Weekly Republican* and the *Weekly Herald*, 26 October 1866, pp. 367-368.

51. Williams, p. 9.

52. *The Philadelphia Photographer* (December 1866), pp. 367-368; letter of 29 July.

53. *The Philadelphia Photographer* (June 1867), p. 194.

54. Taft, 1938, p. 280. See also William D. Pattison, "The Pacific Railroad Rediscovered," *Geographical Review* 53 (January 1962), pp. 25-36. Woodengravings after Russell's photographs were published in *Leslie's Illustrated Weekly Magazine*, 10 May 1869. I am indebted to Van Deren Coke for supplying certain biographical information on Russell drawn from military records in the NA. Russell applied for an invalid pension in 1891, stating his age as 61, which indicates a birth date of 1830. He was a resident of Brooklyn in 1891 and was declared to have failing eyesight and to be suffering from senility. Military records show that he died

in 1902. Coke's data suggests that Pattison, in dating Russell's death in 1896, was incorrect.

55. Turrill, p. 29; see also his "List of Alfred A. Hart Stereos C. P. R. R.," Typescript, California State Library, Sacramento, n.d.

56. Watkins stereo no. 133, Missouri State Historical Society.

57. C. R. Savage, "A Photographic Tour of Near 9000 Miles," *The Philadelphia Photographer* (September-October 1867), pp. 287-289, 313-315.

58. W. H. Jackson. Diary, 22 June- 27 September 1869; 1 August-1 November 1870, Manuscript Division, NYPL.

59. Ibid., entries for 21 August and 19 September 1870 recount his meetings with Russell and his printer.

60. Goetzmann and Bartlett describe the goals and structure of the great surveys. The role of photography is discussed in Goetzmann, "Images of Progress, the Camera Becomes a Part of Western Exploration," pp. 603-606; a selection of photographs are reproduced on pp. 606-648. L. F. Schmeckebier, *Catalogue and Index of the Publications of the Hayden, King, Powell and Wheeler Surveys*, Washington, 1904, overlooks entirely the photographs published by the survey, although he lists Jackson's catalogue of negatives.

61. W. H. Jackson, Diary, 21 August and 19 September 1869.

62. J. D. Whitney, *The Yosemite Book*, New York, 1868, describes the founding of Yosemite as a public pleasure ground.

63. Thurman Wilkins, *Clarence King*, New York, 1958, p. 135. Quoted from a letter apparently in the King papers, HEH. Watkins included a photographic facsimile of King's and Gardner's 1865 map of Yosemite in portfolios of Yosemite photographs as in, for example, the NYPL set.

64. Turrill, p. 33.

65. Samuel F. Emmons, Diary, 5 December 1868, Manuscript Division, LC. King spent the season of 1867/1868 in the company of Emmons, and Emmons's enthusiasm for the photographs is suggested in the diligence with which he noted O'Sullivan's progress.

66. David H. Dickason, *The Daring Young Men: The Story of the American Pre-Raphaelites*, Bloomington, Indiana, 1953, describes King's role in the movement.

67. "Report of Operations," Clarence King to Gen. A. A. Humphreys, 18 December 1867, Record Group 77, NA; Lt. G. M. Wheeler to Humphreys, 7 September 1870, Record Group 77, NA.

68. Letter, King to Humphreys, 18 December 1871, Record Group 77, NA.

69. Letter, Wheeler to Humphreys, 24 March 1870, Record Group 77, NA. Wheeler later said in his *Geographical Report: United States Geographical Survey of the Territories*

West of the 100th Meridian, vol. I, Washington, 1889, p. 17, that O'Sullivan "produced a little less than three hundred negatives."

70. (John Carbutt), "Carbutt's Portable Developing Box," *The Philadelphia Photographer* (January 1865), pp. 4-5.

71. The letters and papers of the scientists are fertile material for future research on photographers with the government surveys. Important collections are held at the NA, LC, HEH, Western Americana Collection of YU, and the Department of Special Collections, UCLA. Goetzmann and Wilkins offer further guidance.

72. Clarence King, *Catastrophism and the Evolution of Environment*, Address, Yale College, 20 June 1877, printed keepsake, n.p., n.d.

73. Ibid.

74. Robert L. Herbert, ed., *The Art Criticism of John Ruskin*, New York, 1964, p. 33.

75. G. K. Gilbert, Fieldbook no. 1109, 1871/1872 (a first draft of the theory), Record Group 57, NA.

76. Agassiz's most relevant books are *Methods of Study in Natural History*, Boston, 1863, and *Geological Sketches*, Boston, 1866.

77. Agassiz, 1866, p. 30.

78. William H. Brewer, *Up and Down California in 1860-1864*, New Haven, 1930, p. 258. In a letter to R. W. Rossiter, Brewer said: "On our trip, in 1863, I talked much about the value of large photographs in geological surveys. I had taken a fancy to stereoptical [sic] views especially; and I thought the broken country about Lassen peak should be photographed, and could not be shown satisfactorily by drawings. In later years King was the first to carry out these ideas on a grand scale; and now the camera is an indispensable part of the apparatus of field-work in such surveys. Many similar instances might be given in which King did the things of which others had dreamed," in James D. Hague, *Clarence King Memoirs*, New York, 1904, p. 324.

79. Thomas Starr King, *The White Hills*, Boston, 1866, pp. 7-8. King observed in his preface that he wanted to "arrange the volume by subjects instead of by districts, and to treat the scenery under the heads of rivers, passes, ridges, peaks, &c" in order to accomplish "artistic unity" for the book. Western landscape photographs fall into those categories and would also be receptive to such "iconographical" treatment.

80. Thomas Starr King, *A Vacation in the Sierras—Yosemite in 1860*, ed. John A. Hussey, San Francisco, 1962, p. 61.

81. W. Whitman Bailey, "Recollections of the West Humboldt Mountains," *Appalachia* 4 (July 1884), pp. 151-154 (selections from Bailey's diary, 3 September-4 October 1867, in which his excursions with O'Sullivan are described).

82. Ibid., 7 September 1867: "The scenery from these strange rocks was very fascinating, and the view from them down upon the desert most magnificent."

83. B. P. Avery, "Art Beginnings on the Pacific," *The Overland Monthly* I (August 1868), p. 166; Nancy D. W. Moore, "Five Eastern Artists Out West," *The American Art Journal* V (November 1972), pp. 15-31, deals with the western activities of Sanford R. Gifford (Fig. 92) and Worthington Whittredge (Fig. 24) among others.

84. Lindquist-Cock, 1973, reproduces an example, p. 75 and discusses the influence of Watkins and Muybridge photographs on Albert Bierstadt. Devéria photographs are in the collection of Samuel Wagstaff, Jr., New York.

85. Brother Cornelius, *Keith, Old Master of California*, n.p., 1942, does not mention the relationship between Watkins and Keith, but Watkins's biographer does. Keith's collection of Watkins's photographs is in the collection of UCB. Emily P. B. Hay, *William Keith as Prophet Painter*, San Francisco, 1916, demonstrates the adulation Keith received in his lifetime.

86. "Views in the Yosemite Valley," *The Philadelphia Photographer* (March 1866), p. 106.

87. *Alta California*, 17 February 1868, quoted in Anita V. Mozley, "Photographs by Muybridge, 1872-1880," *Eadweard Muybridge, The Stanford Years*, Exhibition catalogue, SU Museum of Art, 7 October-3 December 1972, p. 39 (Hereafter cited as *Stanford Years*).

88. *Alta California*, n.d., quoted in John S. Hittell, *Yosemite: Its Wonders and Its Beauties*, San Francisco, 1868, p. 61.

89. One such device was the Shives patent solar camera illustrated in *The Philadelphia Photographer* (February 1865), p. 22.

90. A. S. Semmendinger, the camera maker of Fort Lee, New Jersey, patented the hanging device for his mammoth-plate camera for 18 x 21 in. glass-plate holder on 25 November 1873.

91. Muybridge published his design for a "New Sky Shade" in *The Philadelphia Photographer*, May 1869, reprinted in full in Anita Mozley and J. Sue Porter, "Documents," in *Stanford Years*, pp. 110-111.

92. The exchange of letters between Muybridge, Bradley and Rulofson, and Houseworth is reprinted in full ibid., pp. 111-112.

93. F. V. Hayden to director of Academy of Natural Sciences, Philadelphia, 24 July 1876, mounted in album of *Photographs of the Principal Points of Interest in Colorado, Wyoming, Utah, Idaho, and Montana . . . by W. H. Jackson, Photographer to the Survey*, Washington, 1876.

94. Ibid.

95. Oliver Wendell Holmes, "Doings of the Sunbeam," *Atlantic Monthly* 12 (July 1863), p. 8. See also two other articles on the stereograph by Holmes: "Sun-Painting and Sun-Sculpture," *Atlantic Monthly* 8 (1861), pp. 13-29, and "The Stereoscope and the Stereograph," *Atlantic Monthly* 3 (1859), pp. 738-747.

96. James D. Hague, "Memoirs," *Clarence King Memoirs*, New York, 1904, p. 383.

97. Wheeler Survey Records; Letter, O'Sullivan to Wheeler, 11 November 1875, Western Americana Collection, YU. O'Sullivan was living at 36 Calvert St., Baltimore, according to G. K. Gilbert's address book, Fieldbook no. 3378, NA.

98. The most obvious depositories would be the NA or the LC in Washington, where only incomplete sets of the annual series are held. Several complete sets of the boxed set of fifty are catalogued. On the dispersal of the Wheeler Survey Records see C. E. Dewing, "The Wheeler Survey Records: A Study in Archival Anomaly," *The American Archivist* (April 1964).

99. Letter, Wheeler to Gen. A. A. Humphreys, 1 December 1875, Wheeler Survey Records, Western Americana Collection, YU.

100. Between 1844, when W. H. Fox Talbot's *Pencil of Nature* appeared, and 1859 less than one hundred books illustrated with original photographs are catalogued. Richard Yanul informs me that the first American book illustrated with a photograph is John C. Warren, *Remarks on Some Fossil Impressions in the Sandstone Rocks of the Connecticut River*, Boston, 1854, with a folding salt print. The attempt to illustrate the *Photographic and Fine Art Journal* of 1857 with original photographs was ambitious indeed; see also Fig. 14.

101. Rare Book Room, NYPL; but the 1865 works bear little in common with the UCB salt prints or woodengravings after the 1859 Yosemite views.

102. I am grateful to Elizabeth Glassman for drawing my attention to the importance of the Langford lectures; N. P. Langford, "The Wonders of Yellowstone," *Scribner's Monthly* (May 1871), pp. 1-17; (June 1871), pp. 341-342. Langford accompanied the Washburn Expedition to Yellowstone in 1870. The primary sources of information about the effect of *Yellowstone's Scenic Wonders* on Congress are Jackson's own memoirs and those of his son Clarence. No sets properly identified as the property of a senator or congressman have yet come to light. Nor was Jackson the first ecological photographer; a decade earlier C. E. Watkins's Yosemite photographs, some of which belonged to Senator John Conness, had influenced Congress to cede Yosemite to the state of California.

103. Julian H. Steward, *Notes on Hillers' Photographs of the Paiute and Ute Indians Taken on the Powell Expedition of 1873*, Washington, 1939; Lorraine Dexter, "The Powell Surveys," Typescript, South Woodstock, New York, n.d., is informative and has a useful bibliography; Don D. Fowler *"Photographed All the Best Scenery . . .,"* Salt Lake City, 1972, is an introduction to Hillers's work with Powell.

104. Ralph W. Andrews, *Picture Gallery Pioneers*, New York, 1964, reproduces and describes many of the galleries of the West, the Rocky Mountains, and the Western Plains.

105. Price, Reilly, Walker & Fagersteen, Varela, and Hayward & Muzzall are listed in Darrah, alphabetical checklist.

106. William Henry Jackson *Descriptive Catalogue of the Photographs of the United States Geological Survey of the Territories, for the Years 1869 to 1873, Inclusive*, Washington, 1874.

107. Collier, Weitfle, Gurnsey, Thurlow, and Hines are also listed in Darrah, alphabetical checklist.

108. The trend from art photographs to picture postcards is demonstrated in the career of W. H. Jackson, who became a partner in the Detroit Publishing Co., one of the most successful producers of postcards. Jackson's role is described by Jefferson R. Burdick, *The Handbook of Detroit Publishing Co. Post Cards*, Syracuse, New York, 1954.

109. Collections of Watkins's photographs are in the following institutions: California Historical Society, California State Library, HEH, IMP/GEH, LC, NYPL, SU, United States Geological Survey (Denver), UCB (Hearst Collection and Bancroft Library), UCLA (Research Library). All the collections are carefully described by J. W. Johnson, *The Early Pacific Coast Photographs of Carleton E. Watkins*, Mimeo, Berkeley, 1960. Collections not examined by Johnson include: MMA, Buffalo and Erie County Public Library, Library of Gray Herbarium, HU, BPL, AGS, and the Western Americana Collection of YU.

110. Turrill, p. 30.

111. Woodengravings after Weed's photographs are in *California Magazine and Mountaineer*, May 1860. Some of the original photographs are in the Bancroft Library, UCB.

112. Anthony, *New Catalogue of Stereoscopes and Views . . .* (about 1865), lists views of later manufacture than those published on mounts also bearing a 501 Broadway address.

113. See Weinstein et al., *The American West* 4, pp. 40-49.

114. Dix, pp. 5-25, reprints commentary from the press.

115. "Free exhibition of over six hundred stereoscopic views. Egypt, the Holy Land . . . Portions of the Eastern United States . . . The exhibition free to all—R. H. Vance" (*California Magazine and Mountaineer*, November 1861); see also "Photography in California," *Photographic and Fine Art Journal* (April 1857), pp. 112-113. Of the nine photographers listed, only G. R. Fardon was noted as specializing in outdoor work.

116. Francis Frith, *Egypt and Palestine Photographed and Described*, London, n.d.

117. Holmes, *Atlantic Monthly* 12 (July 1863), p. 8.

118. Brewer, p. 406.

119. *The Philadelphia Photographer* (September 1867), pp. 287-289.

120. W. H. Jackson Diary, September 1869, and Whitney, *The Yosemite Book*, give the clearest idea of the production of a single season. Watkins did not date his photographs, although good records of his life allow a chronology to be deduced. Also useful as aids to dating Watkins's work are lithographs after his photographs in *Geology*, California State Survey, vol. I, 1864.

121. Whitney, *The Yosemite Book*, contains original half-plate photographs from the 1866 season.

122. Ludlow, *The Heart of the Continent*, p. 412. By 1864 Watkins had sold his work to collectors in France and England, where the Earl of Romney purchased a group. Watkins's *Daily Pocket Remembrancer* for 1864 (Bancroft Library, UCB) reveals that he sold a collection of thirty Yosemite views, unmounted, to a Mr. Boyd of Hartford for $130 in gold.

123. *The Philadelphia Photographer* (March 1866), p. 106; (September 1869), pp. 287-289.

124. Turrill, p. 33.

125. Ibid.

126. Clarence King, *Mountaineering in the Sierra Nevada*, New York, 1871. Chap. X describes the ascent of Mt. Shasta in 1870. The spiritual aspects of King's character are evident in the King correspondence at HEH.

127. Biographical sources for King are *Clarence King Memoirs*, New York, 1907, and Thurman Wilkins, *Clarence King*, New York, 1958.

128. Letter, Samuel F. Emmons to "My Dear Arthur," 11 November 1870 (Manuscript Division, LC). When transcribed the letter amounts to thirty-five single-spaced pages and is very informative about King's day-to-day agenda. My thanks to Stephen Feldman for his help with the transcription.

129. T. Wilkins, p. 135.

130. Letter, Watkins to Prof. George Davidson, 2 September 1878 (Bancroft Library, UCB), in which he says, ". . . that thief of a crook got everything away from me, and I don't propose to cry about it. . . ." Watkins's new-series photographs appeared before 1878, and the letter probably retells an old story.

131. Watkins's *Daily Pocket Remembrancer* for 1864 (Bancroft Library, UCB), suggests he had not numbered the negatives before 7 January. After that his entries contain identification numbers, the highest of which is 35 ("Ft. Bragg").

132. Watkins's photographs published by Taber are imprinted with Taber's name only. However, the numbers coincide with those used by Watkins on his old series. The new series included some copied from existing prints of old views reduced to imperial and cabinet size. Because they are reduced from mammoth originals they retain considerable detail, and it is not easy to detect that the negatives are not from nature.

133. Turrill, p. 33.

134. G. K. Gilbert. Fieldbook no. 1971. Record Group 57, NA.

135. Letter, Watkins to Francis Sneed, 26 June 1880, quoted in Ralph W. Andrews, *Picture Gallery Pioneers*, New York, 1864, p. 37.

136. Turrill, p. 33.

137. Ibid.

138. Ibid.

139. Except for an article by John Sampson ("Photographs from the High Rockies," *Harper's Magazine* 39, September 1869), based on an interview with O'Sullivan. The primary sources of biographical information are the archives of the expeditions O'Sullivan accompanied and the notebooks of his companions. The exact date and place of O'Sullivan's birth are unclear, for as Peter Bunnell has pointed out (review of James Horan, *America's Forgotten Photographer: The Life and Work of Timothy O'Sullivan*, New York, 1966, and Beaumont Newhall and Nancy Newhall, *T. H. O'Sullivan, Photographer*, Rochester, 1966, in *Aperture* 13: 2, 1967), the information contained in O'Sullivan's letter of application for the position of photographer to the Treasury Department (Horan, p. 314) and his death certificate (Horan, p. 319), n. 3) are contradictory.

140. Sampson, "Photographs from the High Rockies."

141. Horan, pp. 314-315.

142. No complete set of photographs from the King Survey exists in one location, although the NA has custody of 178 of the original negatives from the King and Wheeler surveys. The NA has part of King's original office set and modern prints from all the negatives (see Figs. 151, 152, Pl. 64). The most complete set is a group of 177 albumen prints in the Department of Prints and Photographs, LC. This set was numbered and captioned a few years after the negatives were made; sets at the IMP/GEH, MIT, the Western Americana Collection of YU, and AGS are without captions, which limits their usefulness. Unlike the photographs from the Wheeler Survey, the King pictures are imprinted with neither numbers nor captions on the mounts, and when the photographs are captioned the information is handwritten. The negatives apparently went through three editions: 1) with no numbers scratched into the emulsions, 2) with numbers scratched in a fine line, 3) with numbers scratched in a coarse line. A few of A. J. Russell's negatives made during his brief stint with the King Survey (Fig. 67, Pl. 94) were published on mounts with O'Sullivan's name and have therefore been considered O'Sullivan's work. Fig. 67 was made at the same time as Russell's variant image, Surveying Under Difficulties (Fig. 177), at YU and is still found on O'Sullivan's mounts at AGS. [W.J.N.]

143. Sampson, "Photographs from the High Rockies."

144. O'Sullivan's negatives from the Wheeler Survey and those of William Bell are intermingled with the King Survey negatives in the NA. The Wheeler Survey must have produced approximately as many negatives (200-plus) as the King Survey, but only fifty of these can be firmly identified because they were issued in bound albums on mounts with the imprint of the Wheeler Survey, each with a number corresponding to the year of issue. Similarly, sets of fifty stereographs were issued annually, and in 1875 a boxed set of fifty selected from the previous four seasons were issued. Sets of the Wheeler Survey photographs are in the collections of the LC, the NA, Western Americana Collection of YU, BPL, NYPL, and the Museum of Natural History, New York [W.J.N.].

145. Correspondence, Lt. George M. Wheeler, Records of the Office of the Chief of Engineers, Record Group 77, NA.

146. G. K. Gilbert. Fieldbooks. Record Group 57, NA, quoted extensively in Horan, p. 246 ff.

147. Walt Whitman, *Specimen Days*, Boston, 1971, in particular "Unnamed Remains the Bravest Soldier," p. 21. (First edition 1882.)

148. Alexander Gardner, *Photographic Sketch Book of the War*, Washington, 1865/1866.

149. Bradley and Rulofson. *Catalogue of Photographic Views . . . by Muybridge*, San Francisco, 1873. The most significant collection of Muybridge's 1867 work is in the Bancroft Library, UCB, where a substantial number of the mammoth-plate Yosemite views can also be found. Other institutions holding the mammoth views include UCLA (Department of Special Collections, Research Library), OM, IMP/GEH, Yosemite National Park Museum, and MMA.

150. Robert Bartlett Haas, "Eadweard Muybridge, 1830-1904," in *Stanford Years*, p. 11. Haas's forthcoming biography of Muybridge can be expected to deal at length on this aspect of the photographer's life.

151. Hood and Haas, p. 7 ff.

152. Ibid., pp. 10-11 print in full Muybridge's advertisement for the 1868 sales campaign.

153. *Stanford Years*, pp. 110-111 reprint the entire article in which Muybridge describes the sky shade (*The Philadelphia Photographer*, May 1869), with linecuts of Muybridge's designs. Anita V. Mozley informs me that some have questioned whether the wooden device is actually a model for the lateral sky shade.

154. Muybridge adopted the Indian names popularized by James Mason Hutchings in his *Scenes of Wonder and Curiosity in California*, San Francisco, 1861. Hutchings's role in founding Yosemite is described by Francis P. Farquhar, *Yosemite, the Big Trees and the High Sierra*, Berkeley and Los Angeles, 1948.

155. Hood and Haas, p. 14.

156. Bradley and Rulofson, p. 11. Gen. A. A. Humphreys gave Lt. George Wheeler permission on 25 May 1869 to hire a photographer out of funds appropriated for surveys for military defense. The photographer he ultimately hired is not mentioned, but since O'Sullivan was at this time working for Clarence King, and would not begin to work for Wheeler until 1871, it is likely that Wheeler hired one of the Bay Area photographers. Both Watkins and Muybridge would have been candidates for the job. Muybridge had spent time around the military establishments, which he recorded in stereographs such as "1670 and 1870 at Alcatraz Island, no. 323." Military views are not found among Watkins's stereographs.

157. *Alta California*, 7 April 1872, quoted in full by Anita V. Mozley, "Photographs by Muybridge, 1872-1880, Catalog and Notes on the Work," *Stanford Years*, p. 45.

158. Elizabeth M. Cock, "The Influence of Photography on American Landscape Painting, 1839-1880," pp. 89-95.

159. Hittell, endpapers (Muybridge advertisement; see Fig. 162).

160. *The Philadelphia Photographer* (February 1864), quoted in full in *Stanford Years*, p. 39.

161. Susan Coolidge, "A Few Hints on the California Journey," *Scribner's Monthly*, May 1873, p. 29.

162. Haas, *Stanford Years*, p. 14.

163. Ibid., p. 18.

164. Eadweard Muybridge, *The Pacific Coast of Central America and Mexico, The Isthmus of Panama; Guatemala; and the Cultivation and Shipment of Coffee, Illustrated by Muybridge*, San Francisco, 1876, which documents Muybridge's Central American trip, exists in a very small edition, each volume slightly different. Examples can be seen at MOMA, and Bender Rare Book Room and Department of Special Collections, SU.

165. In a letter to Leland Stanford (2 May 1892, Bancroft Library, UCB) Muybridge summarized his work photographing the stages of the horse's stride. Quoted in full in Haas, *Stanford Years*, pp. 128-129.

166. Françoise Forster-Hahn, "Marey, Muybridge and Meissonier, the Study of Movement in Science and Art," *Stanford Years*, pp. 85-109, describes Muybridge's influence and activity abroad.

167. *Anthony's Photographic Bulletin* 1 (1870), pp. 33-35. [See n. 54 for further biographical information.]

168. Ibid., p. 34.

169. Marjorie C. Frost, *Nunda News*, 18 September 1969, pp. 1, 5. The full text of four letters was made available by Ms. Frost.

170. Reports of Russell's activities are in *The Philadelphia Photographer* 6 (1869), p. 89; 7 (1870), pp. 82-83.

171. *Nunda News*, 18 September 1869, pp. 1, 5.

172. *Nunda News*, 29 May 1869. The tone of the letter reflects the pomposity of the ceremony at Promontory, but Russell's style of writing is as spirited as in the other letters he sent to the newspaper that summer.

173. L. Thomas Frye, Curator of History, The Oakland Museum, generously arranged for me to study the plates and related materials and discussed with me the introduction to the second edition of Combs, *Westward to Promontory*. Susan Burns put lists of titles and notes on Russell's plate-numbering system at my disposal. [The largest collection of albumen prints from the negatives is in the Western Americana Collection, YU. These approximately two hundred prints were made in the 1870s or 1880s. Prints contemporaneous with the negatives are found in *The Great West Illustrated* (New York, 1869), each volume containing fifty photographs. Examples have been located in BPL; Western Americana Collection, YU (two copies); and HEH. Van Deren Coke has in his collection a version with ms notes.—W.J.N.]

174. In his letter of 3 July 1869 Russell described the Indian settlement near the Weber River, where he received permission to photograph.

175. Letter, *Nunda News*, August 1869.

176. Certain prints from Russell's negatives appear on the mounts of the King Survey under O'Sullivan's name (Fig. 67, Pl. 94).

177. William Pattison, *The Geographical Review* 53, no. 1 (1962), pp. 25-36.

178. Taft, 1938, pp. 272, 281. Robert Taft, *Artists and Illustrators of the Old West, 1850-1900*, New York, 1953, p. 310. Information on Russell's life is scanty, but much of what is known concerns his photographic career, particularly the confusion of authorship among work by Russell, C. R. Savage, and Stephen J. Sedgwick. Pattison (*The Geographical Review* 53) explains the history of the Promontory misattribution.

179. Letter, Russell to Sedgwick, on Leslie's letterhead (8 April 1876, Sedgwick Collection, Department of Special Collections, UCLA): "As Mr. Leslie wishes to use it in the paper. . . . Friend Sedgwick is requested to send either a print or the negative of a picture I took from the top of the Mormon Tabernacle looking towards camp Douglas. . . ." (signed) A. J. Rusell [sic].

180. W. H. Jackson, *Time Exposure, the Autobiography of William Henry Jackson*, New York, 1940, pp. 25, 73.

181. Many drawings are reproduced in Clarence S. Jackson, *Picture Maker of the Old West, William H. Jackson*, New York, 1947, pp. 1-6.

182. W. H. Jackson, *Time Exposure*, p. 173.

183. Ibid., pp. 172-173.

184. W. H. Jackson, Diary, 24 June 1869. On Hull's later work, see Nina Hull Miller, *Shutters West*, Denver, 1962, pp. 11-16. Hull arrived in Omaha in 1866 a more experienced photographer than Jackson.

185. W. H. Jackson, Diary, 27 August 1869.

186. William Henry Jackson, *Descriptive Catalogue* . . . . The 1874 edition lists Jackson's own photographs to that date and includes the collection of ethnographic photographs donated to the Smithsonian Institution by William Blackmore. The catalogue numbers are usually scratched in the emulsions.

187. W. H. Jackson, Diary, 29 June 1869.

188. Ibid., 26 July, 21 August, 19 September 1869.

189. W. H. Jackson, *Time Exposure*, p. 191.

190. No album or collection of the 1872 Yellowstone photographs has been positively identified among the papers of a senator or congressman. The question of exactly how Jackson's photographs were presented to Congress deserves further investigation.

191. W. H. Jackson, *Time Exposure*, pp. 64-83.

192. Beaumont Newhall and Diana Edkins, *William H. Jackson*, New York and Fort Worth, 1974, documents Jackson's postexpeditionary career more thoroughly than any other source; pp. 157-158 list the major collections of Jackson photographs. The mammoth-plate views of the 1880s are rare in public collections.

193. W. H. Jackson, *Time Exposure*, p. 186.

Selected bibliography

Agassiz, Louis. *Geological Sketches*. Boston, 1866.

Agassiz, Louis. *Methods of Study in Natural History*. Boston, 1863.

Anderson, Ralph H. "Carleton E. Watkins, Pioneer Photographer of the Pacific Coast." *Yosemite Nature Notes* XXXII (April 1953), pp. 34-39.

Andrews, Ralph W. *Picture Gallery Pioneers*. New York, 1964.

Anthony, E. and Anthony, H. T. *New Catalogue of Stereoscopes and Views Manufactured and Published by E. & H. T. Anthony & Co., Emporium of American and Foreign Stereoscopic Views*. New York, n.d.

Avery, B. P. "Art Beginnings on the Pacific." *The Overland Monthly* I (July 1868), pp. 28-34; (August 1868), pp. 113-119.

Bailey, W. W. "The Springs of the Great Basin." *Appleton's Journal of Literature, Science and Art*, 22 July 1871.

Bailey, W. Whitman. "Recollections of the West Humboldt Mountains." *Appalachia* 4 (1884), pp. 151-154.

Bartlett, Richard A. *Great Surveys of the American West*. Norman, Oklahoma, 1962.

Baumhofer, Hermine M. "T. H. O'Sullivan." *Image*, vol. 2 (April 1953).

Bendix, Howard E. "The Stereographs of Albert Bierstadt." *Photographica* (September, October, November 1974; January 1975).

Bourne and Shepherd. *A Permanent Record of India*. Calcutta, n. d.

Bowles, Samuel. *Our New West*. Hartford, New York, Chicago, 1869.

Bradley & Rulofson. *Catalogue of Photographic Views Illustrating the Yosemite, Mammoth Trees, Geyser Springs, and other Remarkable and Interesting Scenery of the Far West, by Muybridge*. San Francisco, 1873.

Brewer, William H. *Up and Down California in 1860-1864*. New Haven, 1930.

Brewster, Sir David. *The Stereoscope: Its History, Theory and Construction*. London, 1856.

Bunnell, Peter C. Review of *Timothy O'Sullivan: America's Forgotten Photographer*, by James D. Horan. New York, 1966; and *T. H. O'Sullivan, Photographer*, by Beaumont and Nancy Newhall, with an appreciation by Ansel Adams, Rochester, 1966, *Aperture* 13:2 (1967).

Burdick, Jefferson R. *The Handbook of Detroit Publishing Co. Post Cards*. Syracuse, New York, 1954.

Carico, Nellie C. "List of the Hillers Photographs in Albums I, II, III, IV and V of the Powell Survey." Typescript list with annotations. Record Group 57, National Archives, Washington, 1968.

Century Association. *Clarence King Memoirs*. New York, 1904.

Cock, Elizabeth M. "The Influence of Photography on American Landscape Painting, 1839-1880." Unpublished Ph.D. dissertation, New York University, Institute of Fine Arts, 1967.

Combs, Barry B. *Westward to Promontory*. Palo Alto, California, 1969.

Cone and Relyea. *Sun Pictures of Yosemite*. Chicago, 1874.

Coolidge, Susan [Sarah Chauncey Woolsey]. "A Few Hints on the California Journey." *Scribner's Monthly*, vol. VI (May 1873), pp. 25-31.

Cornelius, Brother. *Keith, Old Master of California*. n. p. 1942.

Crofutt, George A. *Crofutt's New Overland and Pacific Coast Guide*. Chicago, 1879.

Darrah, William Culp. *Stereo Views: A History of Stereographs in America and their Collection*. Gettysburg, Pennsylvania, 1964.

Dellenbaugh, Frederick S. *A Canyon Voyage, the Narrative of the Second Powell Expedition . . . in the Years 1871 and 1872*. New York and London, 1908.

Dewing, C. E. "The Wheeler Survey Records: A Study in Archival Anomaly," *The American Archivist* (April 1964).

Dexter, Lorraine. "The Powell Surveys." Typescript. South Woodstock, New York, n. d.

Dexter, Lorraine. "Stereoscopic Photography in California." Typescript. South Woodstock, New York, n. d.

Dickason, David H. *The Daring Young Men: The Story of the American Pre-Raphaelites*. Bloomington, Indiana, 1953.

Dix, John Ross. *Amusing and Thrilling Adventures of A California Artist While Daguerreotyping A Continent*. Boston, 1854.

Doremus, Charles. "Photography at Vienna." *Reports of the Commissioners. . . .* Washington, 1873 (?).

Durand, Asher B. Papers. Manuscript Division, New York Public Library.

Edkins, Diana. *Landscape and Discovery*. Exhibition catalogue. The Emily Lowe Gallery, Hofstra University, 29 January-7 March 1973.

Emerson, Ralph Waldo. *Nature*. Boston, 1836.

Emmons, S. F. Papers. Manuscript Division, Library of Congress, Washington.

Fardon, G. R. *San Francisco Album. Photographs of the Most Beautiful and Public Buildings of San Francisco*, n. d. (about 1856).

Farquhar, Francis P. *Yosemite, the Big Trees and the High Sierra*. Berkeley and Los Angeles, 1948.

Fenton, Roger. *Conway in the Stereoscope*. London, 1860.

Finny, W. C. *Eadweard James Muybridge*. Kingston-Upon-Thames, England, 1937.

Fowler, Don D., ed. *"Photographed all the Best Scenery," Jack Hillers's Diary of the Powell Expeditions, 1871-1875*. Salt Lake City, 1972.

Frith, Francis. *Egypt and Palestine Photographed and Described*. London, n. d. [photographs dated 1857].

Frith, Francis. *"Queen's Bible.* 2 vols. Edinburgh, 1862.

Gardner, Alexander. *Photographic Sketch Book of the War*. Washington, 1865/1866.

Gernsheim, Helmut and Gernsheim, Alison. *The History of Photography*. London, 1969.

Giffin, Helen S. "Carleton E. Watkins: California's Expeditionary Photographer." *Eye to Eye*, no. 6 (September 1954), pp. 26-32.

Gilbert, G. K. Fieldbooks. Record Group 57, National Archives, Washington.

Goetzmann, William H. *Exploration and Empire*. New York, 1966.

Hague, James D. "Memoirs," *Clarence King Memoirs*. New York, 1904.

Hague, James D. *Mining Industry* (with Geological Contributions by Clarence King). Washington, 1870.

Hardwich, T. F. *A Manual of Photographic Chemistry, including the Pratice of the Collodion Process*. New York, 1858.

Haupt, A. Album of photographs of Civil War views by A. J. Russell with printed captions and ms notations. Department of Prints and Photographs, Library of Congress, Washington, n. d.

Hay, Emily P. B. *William Keith as Prophet Painter*. San Francisco, 1916.

Hayden, F. V. *Sun Pictures of Rocky Mountain Scenery. With a Description of the Geographical and Geological Features . . . Containing Thirty Photographic Views along the Line of the Pacific Railroad, from Omaha to Sacramento*. New York, 1870.

Hendricks, Gordon. "The First Three Western Journeys of Albert Bierstadt." *Art Bulletin* 46 (September 1964), pp. 333-365.

Herbert, Robert L., ed. *The Art Criticism of John Ruskin*. New York, 1964.

Heyman, Therese Thau. *Mirror of California: Daguerreotypes*. Exhibition Catalogue. The Oakland Museum, 6 November 1973-27 January 1974.

Himmelfarb, Gertrude. *Darwin and the Darwinian Revolution*. Garden City, New York, 1962.

Hittell, John S. *Yosemite: Its Wonders and its Beauties*. San Francisco, 1868.

Holmes, Oliver Wendell. "Doings of the Sunbeam." *Atlantic Monthly* 12 (July 1863), pp. 1-18.

Holmes, Oliver Wendell. "The Stereoscope and the Stereograph." *Atlantic Monthly* 3 (1859), pp. 738-747.

Holmes, Oliver Wendell. "Sun-Painting and Sun-Sculpture." *Atlantic Monthly* 8 (1861), pp. 13-29

Hood, Mary V. "Charles L. Weed, Yosemite's First Photographer." *Yosemite Nature Notes* 38 (1959).

Hood, Mary V. Jessup and Haas, Robert Bartlett. "Eadweard Muybridge's Yosemite Valley Photographs, 1867-1872." *California Historical Society Quarterly* 52, no. 1 (March 1963), pp. 5-26.

Houseworth, Thomas and Co. *Catalogue of Photographic Views of Scenery On the Pacific Coast and Views in China and Japan*. 5th ed. San Francisco, 1869.

Houseworth, Thomas and Co. *Pacific Coast Scenery*. San Francisco, n. d. (about 1870).

Horan, James D. *Timothy O'Sullivan: America's Forgotten Photographer*. New York, 1966.

Hutchings, James Mason. *Scenes of Wonder and Curiosity in California*. San Francisco, 1861.

Huth, Hans. *Nature and the American: Three Centuries of Changing Attitudes*. Berkeley, 1957.

Humphrey, A. A. Correspondence regarding Wheeler, King, O'Sullivan, and Watkins. Records of the Chief of Engineers. Record Group 77, National Archives, Washington.

Huntington, David C. *The Landscapes of Frederic Edwin Church: Vision of an American Era*. New York, 1966.

Jackson, Clarence S. *Picture Maker of the Old West, William H. Jackson*. New York, 1947.

(Jackson, W. H.) *Ancient Ruins in Southwestern Colorado. Report of the Ancient Ruins Examined in 1875 and 1877*. n. p., n. d.

Jackson, W. H. *Catalogue of Stereoscopic, 6 x 8 and 8 x 10 Photographs by Wm. H. Jackson*. Washington, 1871.

Jackson, W. H. Diary. 22 June-27 September 1869; 1 August-1 November 1870. Manuscript Division, New York Public Library.

Jackson, W. H. *Photographs of the Principal Points of Interest in Colorado, Wyoming, Utah, Idaho, and Montana, from negatives taken in 1869, '70, '71, '72, '73, '74, and '75 by W. H. Jackson, Photographer to the Survey*. Washington, 1876.

Jackson, W. H. *Time Exposure, the Autobiography of William Henry Jackson*. New York, 1940.

Jackson, William Henry. *Descriptive Catalogue of the Photographs of the United States Geological Survey of the Territories, for the Years 1869 to 1873, Inclusive*. Washington, 1874.

Johnson, J. W. *The Early Pacific Coast Photographs of Carleton E. Watkins*. Mimeo. Water Resources Center, University of California, Berkeley, 1960.

Johnson, J. W. "Historic Photographs and the Coastal Engineer." *Shore and Beach* (April 1961).

(Jones, J. Wesley.) "Jones' Pantoscope of California." *California Historical Society Quarterly* 6 (1927), p. 109 ff.

Jordan, David Starr and Jordan, Jesse Knight. "Louis Agassiz, 1807-1873." *Dictionary of American Biography*. New York, 1928.

King, Clarence. *Catastrophism and the Evolution of Environment*. n. p., n. d. (New Haven, 1877?).

King, Clarence. *Mountaineering in the Sierra Nevada*. New York, 1871.

King, Clarence. Papers. Henry E. Huntington Library and Art Gallery, San Marino, California.

(King, Clarence.) *Records of the Geological Exploration of the Fortieth Parallel*. Record Group 57, National Archives, Washington.

King, Clarence. *Three Lakes: Marian, Lall, and Jan and How They Were Named*. New York, 1870.

King, Thomas Starr. *A Vacation in the Sierras—Yosemite in 1860*. Ed. John A. Hussey. San Francisco, 1962.

King, Thomas Starr. *The White Hills*. Boston, 1866 (first ed. 1859).

Knox, Thomas J. "Across the Continent. Overland Scenes." *Leslie's Illustrated Weekly Magazine*, 5 March, 12 March, 19 March, 28 March 1870.

Langenheim, W. . . . *Catalogue of Langenheim's Stereoscopic Pictures on Glass and Paper . . . Made and sold by the "American Stereoscopic Company."* Philadelphia, 1861.

Langford, N. P. "The Ascent of Mount Hayden." *Scribner's Monthly*, vol. VI (June 1873), pp. 129-151.

Langford, N. P. "The Wonders of Yellowstone." *Scribner's Monthly* (May 1871), pp. 1-17; (June 1871), pp. 341-342.

Lindquist-Cock, Elizabeth. "Frederic Church's Stereographic Vision." *Art in America* 61, no. 5 (1973), pp. 70-75.

Lindquist-Cock, Elizabeth. "Stereoscopic Photography and the Western Paintings of Albert Bierstadt." *The Art Quarterly* 33 (1970), pp. 360-378.

Ludlow, Fitz Hugh. *The Heart of the Continent*. New York, 1870.

Mangan, Terry Wm. *Jackson's Colorado Negatives*. State Historical Society of Colorado, 1974.

Miller, Nina Hull. *Shutters West*. Denver, 1962.

Moore, Nancy Dustin Wall. "Five Eastern Artists Out West." *The American Art Journal* V (November 1972), pp. 15-31.

Morton, H. J. "Yosemite Valley." *The Philadelphia Photographer* (December 1866), pp. 376-379.

(Muybridge, E. J.) *Helios Flying Studio—Edw. J. Muybridge*. (Five albums containing stereo halves numbered in manuscript.) Bancroft Library, University of California, Berkeley.

Muybridge, Eadweard. *The Pacific Coast of Central America and Mexico, the Isthmus of Panama; Guatemala; and the Cultivation and Shipment of Coffee, Illustrated by Muybridge*. San Francisco, 1876.

Muybridge, Eadweard J. *Animal Locomotion*. 11 vols. Philadelphia, 1887.

Newhall, Beaumont and Edkins, Diana. *William H. Jackson*. New York and Fort Worth, 1974.

Newhall, Beaumont and Newhall, Nancy. *Masters of Photography*. New York, 1958.

Newhall, Beaumont and Newhall, Nancy. *T. H. O'Sullivan, Photographer*. Rochester, 1966.

Nordhoff, Charles. *California: A Book for Travellers and Settlers*. New York, 1873.

(O'Sullivan, T. H.) "Geological Exploration of the Fortieth Parallel. Clarence King, Geologist-in-charge. Photographs by T. H. O'Sullivan." Typescript list of original photographs. Manuscript Division, Library of Congress, Washington, n. d.

(O'Sullivan, T. H. ?) Sampson, John. "Photographs from the High Rockies." *Harper's Magazine*, vol. 39 (September 1869).

(O'Sullivan, T. H.) "Scenery of Nevada." *Appleton's Journal of Literature, Science and Art*, 27 May 1871, pp. 616-618.

(O'Sullivan, T. H.) "Snake River, Idaho." *Appleton's Journal of Literature, Science and Art*, 3 June 1871.

Pattison, William D. "Westward by Rail with Professor Sedgwick: A Lantern Journey of 1873." *Historical Society of Southern California Quarterly* 42 (1960), pp. 335-349.

Pattison, William D. "The Pacific Railroad Rediscovered." *Geological Review* 53, no. 1 (1962), pp. 25-26.

Richardson, Albert D. *Beyond the Mississippi*. Hartford, 1867.

Rideing, William H. *A-Saddle in the Wild West*. New York, 1879.

Root, M. A. *The Camera and Pencil; or the Heliographic Art*. Philadelphia and New York, 1864.

Rudisill, Richard. *Mirror Image*. Albuquerque, 1971.

Russell, A. J. Letter to editor. *Anthony's Photographic Bulletin* 1 (1870), pp. 33-45.

Russell, A. J. *The Great West Illustrated. Union Pacific Railroad West from Omaha*. New York, 1869.

Russell, A. J. Letter to *The Philadelphia Photographer*, 1869, p. 70; 1870, pp. 82-83.

Sachse, Julius F. "Philadelphia's Share in the Development of Photography." *Journal of the Franklin Institute*, April 1893, pp. 284-286.

Savage, C. R. "A Photographic Tour of Near 9000 Miles." *The Philadelphia Photographer*, September-October 1867, pp. 287-289, 313, 315.

Schmeckebier, L. F. *Catalog and Index of the Publications of the Hayden, King, Powell and Wheeler Surveys*. Washington, 1904.

Sellers, Coleman. "An Old Photographic Club." *Anthony's Photographic Bulletin*, 26 May-10 November 1888.

Stanford University Museum of Art. *Eadweard Muybridge: The Stanford Years, 1872-1882*. Exhibition catalogue, 7 October-3 December 1972. Contributions by Anita V. Mozley, Robert B. Haas, and Françoise Forster-Hahn.

Steward, Julian H. *Notes on Hillers' Photographs of the Paiute and Ute Indians Taken on the Powell Expedition of 1873*. Washington, 1939.

Stokes, I. N. Phelps. *The Hawes-Stokes Collection of American Daguerreotypes by Albert S. Southworth and Josiah Johnson Hawes*. New York, 1939.

Taft, Robert. *Artists and Illustrators of the Old West, 1850-1900*. New York, 1953.

Taft, Robert. *Photography and the American Scene*. New York, 1938.

Thayer William. *Marvels of the New West*. Norwich, Connecticut, 1891.

Thomson, John, ed. *A History and Handbook of Photography*. New York, 1877.

Turner, Frederick J. "The Significance of the Frontier in American History." *Annual Report of the American Historical Association for the Year 1893*. Washington, 1894, pp. 199-227.

Turrill, Charles B. "An Early California Photographer, C. E. Watkins." *News Notes of California Libraries* 13, no. 1 (January 1918), pp. 29-37.

Turrill, Charles B. "List of Alfred A. Hart Stereos—C. P. R. R." Typescript. California State Library, Sacramento. n. d.

Van Tramp, John C. *Prairie and Rocky Mountain Adventures, or Life in the West*. Columbus, Ohio, 1866.

"Views in the Yosemite Valley," *The Philadelphia Photographer* (April 1866), pp. 106-107.

Vischer, Edward. *Pictorial of California*. San Francisco, 1870. Illustrated with photographs by Watkins, Muybridge, and Houseworth.

Warren, John C. *Remarks on Some Fossil Impressions in the Sandstone Rocks of the Connecticut River*, Boston, 1854.

Watkins, C. E. *Daily Pocket Remembrancer*, 1864. Bancroft. Library, University of California, Berkeley.

Watkins, C. E. Letters. Bancroft Library, University of California, Berkeley.

Weinstein, Robert A. "Gold Rush Daguerreotypes." *The American West* IV (August 1967), pp. 33-39, 71-72.

Weinstein, Robert, et al. "In San Francisco and the Mines, 1851-1856." *The American West* 4 (August 1967), pp. 40-49.

Wheeler, Lt. George M. *Geographical Explorations and Surveys West of the 100th Meridian*. Boxed set of fifty stereographs by William Bell and Timothy O'Sullivan. Washington, 1874.

Wheeler, Lt. George M. *Geographical Report: United States Geographical Survey of the Territories West of the 100th Meridian*. vol. I, Washington, 1889.

Wheeler, Lt. George M. Records of the United States Geographical Surveys West of the 100th Meridian. Record Group 77, National Archives, Washington.

Wheeler, Lt. George M. Records of the United States Geographical Surveys West of the 100th Meridian. Western Americana Collection, Beinecke Rare Book and Manuscript Library, Yale University, New Haven.

Whitney, J. D. "Report and Progress of the Field Work from 1860 to 1864." *Geology*, 1865.

Whitney, J. D. *The Yosemite Book. A Description of the Yosemite Valley and Adjacent Region of the Sierra Nevada and the Big Trees of California*. New York; Julius Bien, by the authority of the Legislature of California, 1868.

Wilkins, J. Warrington. "Our Art Possibilities." *The Overland Monthly* II (March 1869), pp. 248-254.

Wilkins, Thurman. *Clarence King*. New York, 1958.

Williams, Henry T. *Williams' Illustrated Trans-Continental Guide of the Pacific Railroad, Scenery of the Far West....* New York, 1876.

Index of personal names